Staging Modern
Playwrights

Staging Modern Playwrights

From Director's Concept to Performance

Sidney Homan

Lewisburg
Bucknell University Press

Associated University Presses
2010 Eastpark Boulevard
Cranbury, NJ 08512

The paper used in this publication meets the requirements of the American National Standard for Permanence of Paper for Printed Library Materials Z39.48-1984.

Library of Congress Cataloging-in-Publication Data

Homan, Sidney, 1938–
    Staging modern playwrights : from director's concept to performance /
Sidney Homan.
        p.   cm.
Includes bibliographical references and index.
ISBN 0-8387-5563-1 (alk. paper)
1. Theater—Production and direction.   2. Drama—20th century—History
and criticism.   I. Title.

PN2053.H63   2003
792'.0233—dc21   2003007542

SECOND PRINTING 2004

PRINTED IN THE UNITED STATES OF AMERICA

to Norma, David, Danny, and our "other boy," Brian

"I was hoping he might shed a little light on my lifelong pre-
occupation with horses' buttocks."
    —Maddie Rooney, in Beckett's *All That Fall*

Contents

Preface: A Double Life

I LEAD A DOUBLE LIFE, ON THE STAGE AND IN THE STUDY, AS AN ACTOR and a director in professional and university theatres and as a scholar and teacher on college campuses. The subject of this performance criticism, therefore, is my own work in the theatre. And other less well-defined theatres, as well. Doing Beckett's *Come and Go* at a retirement center and in the People's Republic of China. A prison tour with his *Waiting for Godot*. A performance of Albee's *Zoo Story* in the courtyard of an apartment complex where the police, confusing the performance with reality, interrupted the final moment when Peter stabs Jerry on the park bench. Guerilla theatre in front of draft boards during the protest years of the 1960s. A play called *Boston Baked Bean*, its dialogue essentially a transcript of the salty talk overheard in a coach's office, which we staged in bars, a public hall, and a detention center, as well as theatres. Pinter's *A Kind of Alaska* before an audience of physicians, who took to heart the character of Hornby, the doctor who has awakened Deborah from a twenty-nine-year coma with an injection of the drug LaDopa. Ionesco's *Rhinoceros* before an audience that included two survivors of Hitler's concentration camps who could understand the hero Berenger in a way that dwarfed whatever I had learned about that character. And hundreds of performances with an improv group, Strike Force, in "found spaces."

With Chapter 1, I try to begin at the beginning, as the director in developing his or her concept of the play comes to terms with the playwright's text. What were the playwright's intentions? How can we know them, or rather, how well can we know them? To what degree does the director become a collaborator with the playwright, a fellow "author" of the text? From questions of intentions I move in Chapter 2 to working with actors as they make their own discoveries about the play, thereby joining the director as one of those fellow collaborators. Chapter 3 talks about the influence of the set on the actors during that period of discovery, and later on the audience during performance. In parallel fashion, Chapter 4 concerns the influence of props on the actor and the performance, with specific reference to the use of the tape re-

9

corder in Beckett's *Krapp's Last Tape*. Chapter 5 and 6 are a pair, the first talking about how the actor builds a history for the character, the second about playing the subtext. In Chapter 7 I relate an experience creating a play, *More Letters to the Editor*, from materials in the real world. In chapters 8 and 9, I move out into the house, first with strategies intended to engage the audience and then performing before what I call "different audiences." In the Notes and Pertinent Sources I express my debt to all those working onstage and in the study, for whose observations and insights I remain forever grateful.

Acknowledgments

In earlier books published by the Bucknell University Press I first recounted some of my experiences directing Pinter, Brecht, and Beckett: *Pinter's Odd Man Out: Staging and Filming "Old Times"; The Audience As Actor and Character; and Beckett's Theaters: Interpretations for Performance*. Here I occasionally expand on ideas first expressed there and, at times, refashion sections of the prose.

Most of all, I am grateful to the actors, directors, and staff of the Acrosstown Repertory Theatre who give me the chance to do on stage, as a director and actor, what I teach and write about on campus.

Staging Modern
Playwrights

1

The Playwright's Intentions

FIDELITY TO WHAT THE PLAYWRIGHT INTENDED INVOLVES NOT JUST
aesthetic, ethical, or even legal questions but also the issue of the
boundaries of interpretation itself. The playwright's text may be a production's heart and soul, the center of all activity, but surely the playwright is not the only creative person involved in the final enactment
onstage. The issue here is: how *creative* can, or should the director be?

The most conservative position — let us call it "the far right" — would
hold that directors and actors merely bring the playwright's text to the
stage, doing just what is supposedly there, or implied in the dialogue,
not to mention stage directions, character notes, as well as instructions
for setting, lighting, or music. Limiting, even demeaning to the director,
as well as actors, I think this position is at length untenable. Unless
the playwright is there at rehearsals, providing an imprimatur for every
decision, every choice, every line reading made by the company, no two
productions, each trying to be faithful to the playwright's intention, can
ever be the same. I beg the obvious here. Some years ago we had a very
distinguished playwright present for two weeks while we rehearsed a
play of his that had not done well in New York.[1] He proved impossible:
charging onstage to contradict, even reprimand the director, refusing to
make a single alteration even though our stage was smaller than the one
in New York, most certainly unwilling to rethink a single moment in a
work that, to be blunt, had been a flop. Even with him present, we
could never do the play as he meant it to be. I am not proud of this but,
to get on with rehearsals, we had to resort to taking turns having drinks
with him at a bar down the street.

But the opposite position — should we call it the "radical left"? —
seems equally untenable, perhaps even unethical. Here, one says "to
hell" with the playwright's text, let alone his or her instructions or intentions, and instead uses the play as nothing more than a jumping-off
place, a dim point of origin. In our day, of course, this decision risks a
legal suit. Beckett took into court a director who, contrary to his wishes,

15

set *Endgame* in a subway, and Pinter lodged an injunction against a production in Rome of *Old Times* when the director insisted that Anna and Kate be played as lesbian lovers (Zinman 1991, 155; Lane 1973, 19–21). Cutting the text, eliminating characters, changing the setting, deleting part of the plot, accommodating the play to the limitations of a particular theater, "rethinking" an older work in terms of modern realities or agendas, making adjustments to be politically correct—these are not uncommon. Still, at times the changes can be flagrant, possibly even illegal. At other times they may be justified by the director's conviction that he or she is legitimately collaborating with the playwright, altering specifics but well within the bounds of the playwright's supposed intentions.

It's easy enough to identify what is flagrant. For example, Nahum Tate in the late seventeenth century tacked a happy ending onto *King Lear*, so that the father did not die, Goneril and Regan confessed their sins, and—wonder of wonder!—Edgar married Cordelia. The 1960s were especially given to updating the classics. Dead playwrights are fair game for this sort of thing. Perhaps honesty is the best policy here: Stoppard did not hide his debt to Shakespeare and, while borrowing seven scenes from *Hamlet*, was clearly writing his own work, "original" in the best sense of the word, when he turned *Hamlet* inside out with his semi-comic *Rosencrantz and Guildenstern Are Dead*. Brecht did likewise with *Coriolanus* and Ionesco with his *Macbett*.

The extremes, then, that radical right and radical left, are clear enough. It is everything in between that is at issue, whenever directors and their theaters announce they are doing a play by such and such an author, are paying royalties to do so, are clearly invoking the name of the playwright. How can we know the playwright's intentions? How *much* can we know of the playwright's intention? Can we define what constitutes a legitimate collaboration between the playwright and the director?

We hardly know the directors, if they even functioned in our sense of the word, of eighteenth-century theater, nor did the term "director's concept" exist until our time. Most likely, the "concept" of a production was up to the leading actors, and while there were several famous directors in the nineteenth century, it was still a time when productions were identified with the lead actor, or actors. But ours is the age of the director, as well as that of the actor. And when it comes to dead playwrights, that reading of intentions has often been stretched to the limit. We have had a Mrs. Lear, or *Hamlet* as a woman, or wholesale lifting of lines from *1 Henry IV* to "improve" its sequel, the less popular *2 Henry IV,* or *Much Ado* set in the ante-bellum South, complete with minstrel songs.[2]

Perhaps two terms from the law might be helpful here. One I have used already: "intention." In matters of legal interpretation that word, of course, refers to what the court perceives as the intentions of the legislature, especially from the distant past. What did the framers of the Constitution *intend* when they said this or that? Or, if lawmakers from the last century had lived today, would they have countenanced a modern re-interpretation of their original statute? What about situations they could not have anticipated? The second term, "realism," defines that school of legal theory arguing against absolute principles, whether it be laws or their interpretation. Instead, the law must be re-examined case by case; every event involves what was called in the 1950s "situational ethics."

I want to relate two personal experiences as director where I thus interpreted the playwright's intent or, when going against the playwright's consciously stated intention, acted on the assumption that the interpretation still fell within the bounds of a permissible collaboration between playwright and director. In light of the two legal terms above, I am concerned with intention as it applies case by case, play by play. My own intention is not to be defensive here, not to prove that I was "right." Those two cases are productions of Pinter's *Old Times* and Shepard's *Curse of the Starving Class.* As something of a musical coda, I conclude with two contrastive instances, one where a playwright otherwise not known for being flexible with directors allows the director and actors almost unlimited latitude (Beckett in his "dramaticule" *Come and Go*), the other an instance where my decision to go against a clear intention was reversed after conversation with the playwright (Eric Bogosian in his *Talk Radio*).

PINTER ON FILM

In 1991 I directed three of my colleagues in the University of Florida Theater Department in both a television and a stage version of Pinter's *Old Times,* my reason for trying the former being to learn more about directing for that medium.[5] Perhaps because my three actors were themselves directors, we started rehearsals eager to fashion an allegorical "grid" for this most mysterious of Pinter's plays. Alas, we came up with one too quickly. Anna, the dinner guest, Kate's friend from their days as young secretaries living together in London, represented the past; Deeley, the husband who, to his mind, has "rescued" Kate from Anna, is the present; and the wife, Kate, the object of their competition this night, is the future. The allegory just as quickly gave us trouble, for with one eye on the lines, and one on this imposed meaning, we couldn't get into the parts. "Let's just play the lines," one of my frustrated actors cried, with another joining in, "And forget all this meaning stuff." This done, rehearsals went smoothly.

In his few recorded comments about the play, Pinter himself seems to support this decision. Avoiding a single interpretation, let alone any attempt at allegory, he observes that "It is all happening," that "it is entirely taking place before your very eyes," in a world where "the past is not past." For the audience, the focus is "Who's feeling what at what time" (Gussow 1971a, 42–43, 126–36).

Still, I could not put away completely this search for some larger meaning. For even with the playwright's own comments about the work's present tense, its theatrical "reality," there are some curious elements in *Old Times*. Anna, for one, stands silently upstage while Deeley and Kate talk about her as if she were not present. And there are two moments in the play (Pinter 1971, 43–44, 62–63) where Kate and Anna, excluding Deeley from the conversation, seem to travel literally back in time to their London days. Even the names of the characters were something of an after-thought, for when Pinter's first wife, the actress Vivian Merchant, read an early draft where Kate, Deeley, and Anna were simply called A, B, and C, she confessed that she could not tell the genders of the three.

And how to account for the almost silent Kate in act 1 suddenly breaking out into two monologues in the second act? The concluding one, delivered with her standing between the slumped figures of Deeley and Anna "dead" on either side, is of a length and verbal complexity unlike anything else in the play (71–73). In a phrase, the play seems at once real and not real.

Deeley and Anna clearly fancy that one of them will "win" Kate this evening; they continually talk about her as if she were an object, a head to be held in one's hands, a prize to be fought over: Anna offering her the lure of sophisticated London, of female bonding; Deeley, the present, marriage, their comfortable life here in "a converted farmhouse" (6) some distance from the city. I began to think: what if, all along, Kate was in charge, was something of a playwright invoking in her dreams these two characters, this woman and man who have figured so prominently in her life? The evening becomes, in effect, a play staged by Kate, where she weighs the competing claims of Anna and Deeley who, as actors unaware, imagine they are real, and that one of them will win her. Even as Pinter himself has already written the play, the fate of Anna and Deeley, beyond their conscious knowledge, is predetermined by what is the enactment of Kate's dream.

Her vision of "living close to the sea," looking through "the flap of a tent and [seeing] sand" (59), suggests a location and a time, the future, beyond Anna's London of the past or Deeley's marital present. In her great final speech (73) Kate speaks of watching Anna's "bones breaking through [her] face" as if she had killed her off. Then she mocks Deeley's own attempts at love-making, before dismissing both of her "suitors" with "Neither mattered."

I had slipped into allegory again, but it was an allegory I wanted to explore, without burdening my actors. And here television proved the perfect medium, given the greater control it affords the director. For with the camera we can to some extent control what the audience sees, and hence the information they receive, in a way impossible onstage.

So I pursued this allegory during the filming by highlighting Kate, especially during that first act where, as my own Kate complained, "I have practically no lines." On film, she became that playwright watching her creations, sharing with the audience emotions otherwise hidden from Anna and Deeley, visually reminding us of her presence. Numerous shots underscored her role as the controlling figure, the dreamer, the puppeteer. I recalled here that record album cover for the musical *My Fair Lady* which pictures Shaw manipulating the strings of his puppets Henry Higgins and Eliza Doolittle.

For example, in the television version at the start of act 1 we see Deeley and Kate from a distance, small figures overwhelmed by the set, as if they were part of it, frozen until Kate's first line "Dark" (7), which ironically is the cue for the stage lights to come up. In the midst of Anna's speech about the man in their room, we cut to Kate as Deeley interrupts with "He'd come back" (33), and kept the focus on her to the pause. When Deeley tries to cancel Kate's question to Anna ("And do you like the Sicilian people?"), the camera remained on Kate, angry at him for this naked display of jealousy (43). As Anna describes Kate's waiting "not just for the first emergency of ripple" (37), we only hear her saccharine line off-screen while on-screen we see Kate deeply affected by the image. Whenever Kate moved to refresh her drink, to light a cigarette at the side table, or to change positions, the camera, while much more stationary with Anna and Deeley, always followed her. I reserved the most elaborate camera work for Kate's final speech; there were in all some eighteen changes in angle and distance. In addition, during post-production work I added close-ups of Kate, sometimes re-acting to a line, often listening, observing. When at one point Anna embarrasses Kate, Pinter's stage direction is *"Kate stares at her"* (43). Our Kate, who has been silent during the shot, rose and conspicuously walked off-camera.

In these ways I could stress the fact that whenever a character thinks he or she is winning, the paradox is that winning Kate is actually losing since the winner/loser axis runs contrary to Kate's larger scenario for the evening. She seems to signal this with her exit in act 1 (46). Feeling victorious, Anna asks Kate if she should draw her bath this evening, as she doubtless has in that past. But Kate, perhaps for this first time, rejects the offer: "No, I'll run it myself tonight." On both screen and stage, Anna, shocked at this display of independence, hurt, turned to watch Kate exiting. Then, feeling Deeley's stare, she turned back to face him, as the husband lifted a glass of brandy, toasting her with the subtext: "You may have won so far, but just now she rejected you. We both heard it. We'll see who wins the rest of the evening."

Predictably, the screen and stage versions were very different. It was the medium of television that allowed me to try out an interpretation that I like to think was supported by the text but which was not fully relevant for my three actors.

An Alternative Ending for Shepard

Sam Shepard's story of the dysfunctional family, *Curse of the Starving Class*, ends with the mother and son, the sole survivors, sharing a story about an eagle and cat locked in mortal combat in midair: "that cat's tearing his chest out, and the eagle's trying to drop him, but the cat won't let go because he knows if he falls he'll die." At length, "they come crashing down to the earth. Both of them come crashing down, like one whole thing" (Shepard 1981, 200). Now critics find here the play's core image for the family's repetitive, hopeless, self-destructive world. The storytelling "signals [the son Wesley's] destruction, his fate, his inheritance from his father" (Randall 1988, 132). The image suggests an "agonistic, almost Strindbergian view of family life, one that sees pain and struggle as inescapable facts of nature" (Wade 1992, 98). The "family [is left] in much the same condition as the eagle and the cat" (Mottram 1997, 138). One commentator argues that Shepard here refuses "to permit unambiguous interpretation," that the image shows "the inescapable influence of heredity," the "primal violence," the "helpless victimization" of Shepard's world [Bottoms 1998, 166, 171–73]. The reader will search far and wide for any variation in this general interpretation. One observer does concede that the story told by Emma and Wesley, which completes even as it varies from the one told by Weston at the start of act 3 (Shepard 1981, 182–84), does distinguish the mother from the father: "She is trapped as the husband. The difference is that the mother does not wallow in defeat" (Tucker 1992, 128–29).

Now, the play *is* bleak, the family self-destructive: Ella has an affair; the father, bankrupt, flees to Mexico to escape two hit men hired by his creditors; Emma, the daughter, robs her sleeping mother and then exits to lead a self-professed life of crime; and the son Wesley goes mad at the end, tearing food from the refrigerator, a victim of his family's "liquid dynamite" (Shepard 1981, 153), their tendency to erupt into violence. Further, the hermetically sealed world of the family is progressively invaded from the outside: by the sleazy owner of a nightclub, the lawyer who seduces the mother, and two crooks who, in our production, were straight out of *Pulp Fiction*. Surely, that closing image of the cat and eagle epitomizes Shepard's world here.

This said, during rehearsals the actors and I also found a small but distinct counter-movement to this pessimism, moments when the family tried to understand each other, experienced tenderness, even sympathy, struggled to be normal, to recreate what must have been blissful days before their decline.[4] The parallel here would be the happy times described by Dodge in *Buried Child*, before the incest which spells the disintegration of that family. Wesley's monologue early in act 1 (137–38) opens with a portrait of the boy lying in his bed, alert to the almost mystical sounds and smells of the larger world outside, before the father's drunken entrance. Even the quarrels, such as over Ella's cooking Emma's chicken (140–41), seem to fall within the bounds of normal family disputes, at least for a while. Drunk as he is, Weston at the end of act 1 still tries to give some fatherly advice to Wesley about caring for the sick lamb onstage (159). Act 2 opens with brother and sister alone, trying to create a family of two. In Emma's words, "Maybe they'll [Ella and her boyfriend Taylor] never come back, and we'll have the whole place to ourselves. We could do a lot with this place" (163). Weston tries to reform his life in act 3: he changes clothes, does domestic chores, cooks for the family. He even has a sentimental conversation with his wife who has returned from staying up all night with Emma at the jail, offering her the table on which to sleep so that she'll wake refreshed as he did (188–89). And we found the final meeting of father and son in act 3 bittersweet, with the father, suddenly realizing the absurdity of his life ("The jumps. I couldn't figure out the jumps"), now appealing to the son for advice (193–96). Such moments only served to highlight that otherwise bleak world. Yet however short-lived, however futile the attempts to reconstitute a normal family, they are there.

This "discovery" led me to change Shepard's stage direction for the ending (200). On the exit of the two crooks, *"Ella is facing downstage now, staring at the lamb carcass in the pen. Wesley has his back to her upstage."* And at the end of the story they mutually tell, the stage direction reads: *"They stay like that with Wesley looking off upstage, his back to Ella, and Ella downstage, looking at the lamb"* as the lights fade. For my actors and me, the ending offered a complex response. While their world may be hopeless, their tragedy of inheritance inescapable (Wesley now wears Weston's clothes), the mother and son *are* together, telling a story together, indeed, invoking the memory of the father who "used to tell about the eagle." Amidst the ruin, at least they can place their world in perspective through this image of the eagle and the cat. A small accomplishment, to be sure, but there, amidst the chaos symbolized by the stage now strewn with food, not to mention overturned chairs and all the detritus of this pathetic household.

Accordingly, we played the moment with a small trace of optimism. On the exit of Slater and Emerson, Wesley was at stage right, facing out, Ella downstage, just as Shepard asks. But on her "Oh! You know what, Wes?" she moved centerstage and sat down on the stage-left side of the table. Wesley was still looking out, shocked by all that has happened, lost in his own thoughts, deeply angry at both parents. His "What" and "Yeah" were barely audible. Ella appealed to him, asking her son to help her remember the story. Gradually, the son's resistance broke down, and on her plaintive "What happens next?" he unfroze, and slowly crossed toward her, at length standing behind his mother who was still seated in the chair. As she began the story, he started to contribute details, mother and son becoming one, a single narrator. With Wesley's most extensive addition to the story, "And that eagle comes down and . . . ," he put his hands gently on her shoulder, lovingly, and she responded to his touch, placing her hand on top of his right hand. Our production ended with mother and son *embracing*, touching physically, acknowledging each other, even as the story they tell invokes the bleakest of images. I had gone against or played a variation on the playwright's stage directions, but in my adding this small victory to his savage portrait of the dysfunctional family I leave it to the reader to determine if I also violated the tenets of those two terms, intentions and realism.

COME AND GO AND TALK RADIO

Ask for permission to stage Beckett's *Endgame* and the publisher will send you a list of requirements that is longer and more detailed than what is normal when contracting for performance rights. No one is more insistent than Beckett when it comes to this issue of the playwright's intentions. And I have found from personal experience that he is absolutely right. Some years ago I did television films of his plays for that medium, following every direction to the letter for *Quad*, *Eh Joe*, . . . *but the clouds* . . . , *Ghost Trio*, and *Nacht und Träume*. But we also filmed what were called "Variations" on three of the works, labeling them clearly as such in the final tape (Homan 1992). Chafing under Beckett's exacting directions, here I used a dissolve where he had called for a fade, there added sound effects in place of his silences, tried different camera angles, even moves: in *Eh Joe* Beckett asks that each move of the camera be exactly three inches closer to his single character seated on the bed. I discovered, however, that Beckett was always right; despite my good intentions, the Variations were always inferior.

This is why his little play *Come and Go* (Beckett 1967, 67–71) is such an exception, an instance where the playwright gives tremendous latitude to director and actors. Three elderly women (Flo, Vi, and Ru) sit on a bench. In rotation, each leaves the bench, is gossiped about by the remaining two, and then returns. While together they speak of the old days, at a Miss Wade's playground where they sat as young girls on a log, holding hands in a daisy-chain pattern, "dreaming of love." Between that time and the present something horrible has happened to each, to the one who exits briefly.

Audiences are used to being omniscient. After all, we hear every word of Hamlet's soliloquy, and as the Director protests in Pirandello's *Six Characters in Search of an Author*, the audience must be aware of every line, even if in real life it was whispered by one character to another. But in *Come and Go* we do not hear the play's most important line, whatever one of the characters tells the other about their absent partner, something so horrible that she whispers with an *"appalled"* look. The first response of the one who hears the bad news is: does the character know of whatever has happened to her? The answer is a plea that she know nothing.

We are used to minimalism in Beckett, and *Come and Go* is no exception. Here the actors wear wide-brimmed hats so that, with the bench lit from directly above and darkness around its periphery, we see the actors' faces only in shadows. Moreover, they wear full-length cloaks so that the entire body is covered. The dialogue is sparse, to say the least. But that missing line goes beyond even this. In what one critic has aptly called "an open silence" (McGuire 1985, xix–xxi), Beckett seems to invite the director, the actors, and most certainly their audiences to supply that unheard line, privately, to our inner self. I have done this play with both professional and amateur actors, and before all types of audiences: senior citizens, academics, children in a Head Start program, a convention of psychiatrists, students, various professions, even in the People's Republic of China. In post-play discussions, when I ask the audience to tell me what they think was whispered, what horrible thing has happened to each of the three women, the answers reveal much about the audience: she is dying of cancer, she is already dead, her husband is cheating on her, she is ugly. A seven-year-old boy speculated that "she has bad breath." At such moments, that word "intention" seems inadequate, even irrelevant. In *Waiting for Godot* the absent character's identity is a veritable black hole inviting each of us to fashion Godot according to our own feelings or needs. Indeed, Beckett has said if he knew who Godot was, he would have said so in the play (Schneider 1958, 3–20). Here, this otherwise strict playwright also invites us to be collaborators. Flo's last line, "I can feel the rings," only sets off another round of speculation—and collaboration.

I end with a contrastive instance where the playwright talked me out of or, more properly, I gladly let him talk me out of making a radical change in his work. In 1991, I directed a production of Eric Bogosian's play *Talk Radio* at the Hippodrome State Theatre, our local Equity house.[5] The central character, Barry Champlain, is a talk-radio host; most of the play involves his chatting with listeners who call the studio. Those callers, some twenty-five in all, represent a cross-section of American society, from the pathetic to the truculent, from racists to die-hard fans, from the agreeable to the disagreeable, from bored housewives to a neurotic caller afraid of "dirty ashtrays" (Bogosian 1988, 48). One, a young fellow named Kent, actually barges into the studio. Barry has been sustained over the years by thinking himself superior to the callers, like a God dispensing advice, wit, humiliating questions, insults. His operator, the assistant producer who is in love with Barry, and his executive producer provide us with biographical information about the host. At the end, disgusted with his job, with himself, Barry dismisses the callers as a "bunch of yellow-bellied, spineless, bigoted, quivering, drunken, insomniatic, paranoid, disgusting, perverted, voyeuristic, little obscene phone callers" (90), only to realize that he and his callers are "stuck with each other" (92).

I had what I thought was a brilliant idea. Why not show the callers? My set designer had given me a very realistic radio studio, with two large windows upstage looking out over the New York skyline at night. What if we put the callers in the sky, a surreal upstage picture balanced by the realistic downstage set? With minimal costume changes (we did the twenty-five callers with five actors), the callers would materialize out of the sky, as if they were waiting there for Barry, hovering just outside the studio windows. My actors loved the idea: they would now be seen as well as heard. Barry wouldn't see them, of course, but the audience would.

However, the theater's Producing Director suggested, rightly, that to avoid any legal complications I call the playwright, or his agent, and ask about this proposed change. I dutifully sent Mr. Bogosian a two-page letter outlining what I wanted to do and saying I would call him a week later, at a time specified by his agent. When I did, we fell quickly into a pleasant discussion about the work. The playwright was not adverse to my idea, although he did point out that all other productions had confined the callers to the theater's sound system. But as we talked I began to see his reasons for not showing the callers, and before the conversation ended I had been *converted* to his view, to his original intention. Showing the callers would violate the realism, the sense of "happening" which informs *Talk Radio*. Not showing them would invite the audience to use its own imagination in fleshing out Rose, Josh, Francine, Junior, Ruth, and the others; it would keep the focus on the play's complex central character. We did the show without showing them. At first disappointed that they would not be seen, my actors quickly came around when I suggested having them double as the onstage characters. In fact, one actor observed that she liked the challenge of creating a character, indeed more than one character, "just using my voice." "Like radio," I added. "Oh, yeah," she replied, "that's from your day." I suddenly felt very old, but also happy that I had not violated the playwright's intentions.

2

Actors and Their Discoveries

IN HER OWN WORDS, SHE "WAS WRETCHED" AT THE AUDITION FOR A production of Wendy Wasserstein's *Uncommon Women and Others* that I was to direct.[1] At the end of the evening, after I was just about to pack up and leave, after three hours of watching hopeful applicants for the seven characters in the playwright's all-woman cast, the actress came out on the empty stage, asking if she could try again. She had waited three hours, wanted another chance, and I threw the theater's rules to the winds and said "yes." This second time, the audition piece was as good as it had been bad the first time. On the way out of the theater, I asked her how long she had been a theater major. "Oh, I'm not. I'm a Music major." "Voice or instrument?" I asked. "I play the saxophone." This literally struck a responsive chord: my dad had been a sax player in B-level "big bands" of the 1920s and 1930s. The next morning her name was on the cast list, to play Carter, the almost silent, non-conformist girl in this play about young women at Wellesley College who, having bonded for four years, now face graduation and entry into a world dominated by men.

In the play Carter mostly stands about, listening, reacting to the other characters, perhaps Wasserstein's symbol of the woman removed from the poles of conformity to a male-dominated world and the challenge of joining the women's movement. Here in this play set in the 1970s the presence of Betty Freidan and Germaine Greer is implied just outside the confines of the small, comfortable college dorm that constitutes the single set. I did notice that my Carter, without lines, was silently mouthing an internal dialogue during the scenes, a subtext buried except as it made its way up through a glance, a change in posture, a gesture. Impressed by her diligence, I asked her if during one scene I might sit next to her and have her whisper to me what she was saying inwardly to herself. What a revelation! She was creating her own play, "the personality under the surface" or "my secret self" as she called it. Little won-

26

der that, even without lines, she was one of the strongest presences onstage, in a cast of excellent actors with lines.

In scene 5 of the first act Carter is discovered alone onstage. Wasserstein's stage direction asks that she "begins ironically to mime modern dance" to the voice of the university president which opens the scene. Then, in the scene's second half, Susie, the play's social butterfly, barges in with elaborate plans to fix Carter up with a date. As Susie exits she hands Carter a valentine card from a "male caller" (Wasserstein 1991, 26–29), so banal that Carter "puts down letter" and ends the scene with an anguished "Gross—me—out!" I offered my Carter a challenge. "Figure out what to do for a minute or so when you're alone." Two rehearsals later she met the challenge. "I've got something to show you in that scene," she promised. Alone onstage, she looked down at the saxophone lying on the sofa beside her. At least for the time being, this was "her man," gentle, quiet, at one with her, and most unlike the other men in the play who remain presences offstage: the stuffy, condescending university president whose remarks, based on the actual inaugural address of Wellesley's first male president, preface each scene; the numerous boyfriends mentioned by the girls, without fail either East Coast snobs or MCPs. Carter picked up the instrument, lovingly, and began playing an old Bunny Berrigan song, "I Can't Get Started," which that evening as we walked from the auditions I had mentioned as my dad's favorite song, indeed, his band's signature song. After eight measures or so, Carter got up and waltzed around the set, the sax her dancing partner. It was a tender moment, "bittersweet" in the words of more than one audience member. Her subtext was something like: "This is as far as I can go now. With relationships. With men. With that world awaiting me on graduation. This is the company I prefer, at least for now."

This was my actor's "discovery," that word actors use to describe a sudden inspiration, a bit of business or delivery that comes to them. Actors often like to think the a discovery emerges out of the blue. I suspect that, in truth, it is the product of a variety of factors: something implicit in the text, a memory or an action from the actor's real-life experience invoked by the text, perhaps an inspiration from the director or a fellow actor. For me, the discovery is that meeting between actor and playwright as fellow collaborators, just as the director in designing a concept for the entire production functions as a co-creator with the playwright. Discoveries can have small, detailed, immediate effects on a show; they can also affect the character's subsequent appearances on stage, even the entire production. For my Carter, her discovery underscored the subtextual signals she had been sending the audience up to this point; it also provided an ironic context, a moment of genuine private feelings, to Susie's clichéd greetings and sophomoric notions of love. It pointed the way for her character in the remaining scenes. Carter was not just withdrawn, not abnormal by any means, no social malcontent, but a young woman biding her time, waiting for her entrance on some larger stage than the confines of an all-woman's college.

The situations for such discoveries are varied. Below I speak in detail about two, one born of frustration, the other from a stray remark by an actor.

"I Feel Like We're Just Floating Free"

"I feel like we're just floating free here. Not connecting." Pamela Greenberg, my Emma in a production of Shepard's *Curse of the Starving Class*,[2] complained to me while we were rehearsing the scene between the brother (Wesley) and sister at the opening of the second act. There had been no problem until this point. In the first act, the brother and sister of Shepard's dysfunctional family quarrel over seemingly routine family matters: Emma's screaming when she discovers the mother, Ella, has cooked a chicken she was going to use in a 4H demonstration; the quarrel was aggravated when both children confront Taylor, who plans to buy their house without the father's knowledge. The two young actors had no trouble connecting in these two scenes; if anything, the quarrels resembled something you might find in a television sitcom. To be sure, *Curse of the Starving Class* would get more complex, more symbolic, even allegorical by the second act, but here in the first act the play, at least on the surface, seemed "a series of good dialogues for actors," as one member of the company termed it.

The opening of act 2 was a different story; it was almost as if *Curse* had shifted into another gear during intermission. I had to agree: the two characters seemed to exist in separate worlds, almost on separate stages. Wesley sat at stage right repairing the door. Emma was at stage center, seated on the stage-left side of the table, redoing her 4H charts on "How to Cut Up a Frying Chicken" that the brother had ruined in act 1 when he urinated on them. (Getting the actor to urinate on cue proved a challenge, which we solved with a "Foley bag" from the university hospital's Department of Urology. But that is another story.) We were only talking about a page of dialogue, yet unable at first to help my actors, I thought to myself: let's just get it over with. Perhaps it will come together later. After that opening page, Emma launches into a long monologue, and when brother and sister re-engage in conversation, again the actors had no problems in connecting. But my Emma wouldn't let go. "What is happening to us here?," she asked.

She was right: the two seem to be talking beyond each other. Emma is worried about what is happening between the mother and her lover, blaming the affair on Ella: "She's after him for his money." When Wesley offers the opposite diagnosis ("He's after our money"), Emma changes the subject with an enigmatic, "She's after more than that." Her diagnosis, "She's after esteem," goes right by Wesley, who changes the direction of the argument by blaming Ella for marrying Weston: this is why she has no esteem, stuck out "here in the boonies." He starts to offer his own reading (both parents "can't think") but Emma cautions, "Don't be too harsh," before abruptly changing the topic with, "How come you didn't tell me when Pop came in last night?" Then, just before her monologue, the conversation, such as there is, appears to fall completely apart as we move from Wesley's "I don't know," to his mentioning that the father brought "dirty laundry," that claim then corrected by Emma's "he brought food." Wesley reminds her the food was just "artichokes," and Emma closes the dialogue with "Better than nothing." After that, she returns to her original concern, Ella and Taylor together, which launches her into the monologue.

Confronted now with two worried actors who wanted this problem solved before going on, I could only plead, "Let's see if the rest of the play tells us how to do this act 2 opening." I had no alternative ideas, but fortunately my actors were content to be content—for a time.

Over the course of the next two weeks we discovered that the play itself is not always that seamless, "naturalistic" series of well-connected dialogues that make life relatively easy for actors in Shepard's plays. *Curse* seems "real" enough on the surface, practically an autobiography of the playwright: Wesley is Shepard, Weston his real-life father, Ella his mother. It has the episodic structure of the "well-made" play: introduction of the four family members, the rising action generated by Weston's plan to sell the house, that action complicated by the arrival of five outsiders, followed by the semi-tragic resolution.

But working against this are non-real, illogical elements that suggest psychological, even allegorical dimensions below the surface. My Wesley, for example, pointed out how early his monologue occurs, before he even has much dialogue with the mother to establish his character. That monologue centers on the details of the father's breaking into the house the night before. "The play just plunges, without warning, into a two-page speech." Furthermore, apparently without motivation Emma calls Taylor "creepy" (Shepard 1981, 21) when he confronts her alone in the kitchen early in the same act. This sequence, before Wesley enters with the lamb, seems like a play in itself, a mutual seduction attempted by both the visitor and the daughter that is somehow aborted.

The language sounds realistic in act 1. But with some hints at the end of act 2 and then full-blown in act 3, it is soon laced with symbols, almost blatant ones, of salvation and rebirth, especially in Weston's monologue at the start of the final act (49–50). Most obvious is the fact that the family's four monologues appear to break free from the play, or to have been dropped into the action. Ella also has a monologue (41), along with Weston's, Wesley's (7–8), and Emma's (30). Indeed, we used special lighting for all four monologues, the general and fairly neutral all-stage lighting giving way to a surreal effect with a green spot for Ella downstage-left, four such spots for father and son covering the entire stage, and a more general downstage area for Emma. Wesley froze during Emma's and Ella's monologues; during Wesley's, Ella stood motionless at the stove. Weston delivered his alone onstage, though I brought in Wesley near the end: he stood silently by the upstage door, listening to his father.

That sitcom atmosphere of the first act itself gives way to actions and characters who are, in a word, *bizarre*. Besides changing into his father's clothes and thereby symbolically underscoring the notion of fate as inherited, Wesley imitates his father by walking naked across the stage, picking up the lamb, and returning sometime later having inexplicably slaughtered it. He claims there is no food, even though in the final act Ella has come back from shopping loaded with groceries. Thus "starving" and "food" join "birth" and "rebirth," not to mention Weston's epiphanies, as motifs which become increasingly powerful as we move from act to act.

Soon, like literary scholars, my Emma and Wesley were given to discourses during rehearsal breaks: about the son's metamorphosing into the father, or Emma's changing radically in the play from a fourteen-year-old experiencing her first period, to a hardened criminal beyond her years as she exits in the final act to pursue her life of crime. Our make-up artist, at Emma's suggestion, made fairly radical cosmetic changes on her between the acts: from a ponytail in act 1, to hair in the style of her mother by act 3, from a girlish complexion, to something mature beyond her years in the final act. She also changed from the youthful 4H uniform to a fashionable riding outfit. We even dressed in outlandish costumes Slater and Emerson, the two hired thugs who come to collect Weston's debt. For me, they called up memories of those surrealistic criminals in Hemingway's short story, "The Killers."

By far the most bizarre action, however, is Wesley's tearing food out of the refrigerator in the final act. Shepard's stage direction is: he "starts pulling all kinds of food out and eating it ravenously" (Shepard 1981, 57). By opening night this direction had evolved into Wesley's tearing open the door, pulling out food, and scattering it all over, until the stage was littered with crackers, corn chips, cereal, and artichokes. He then threw himself onto the floor and began eating like an animal. The audience was always shocked, bolting upright in their seats; some nights food came perilously close to spectators in the first row. The audience would be shocked again by the offstage noise of the car exploding, presumably with Emma in it. Shepard is unclear here, and the scholars and critics I consulted are likewise. We assumed that Emma, trying like her father to escape, has been blown up in the car, the Kaiser-Fraser, which she says she is taking. To clear up any doubts, we had Wesley repeat the brand name, instead of saying just "car," when Emerson and Slater announce what they have done. Full-blast on the theater's sound system, that explosion always startled the audience.

Collecting all these observations, we now saw *Curse of the Starving Class* as actually two plays in one: a moderately realistic family history and an allegory, similar to Shepard's *A Lie of the Mind*, about modern America, the clash between city and country, old values and the present age, the family imperiled by each other and the attending world. Now we could return to that difficult opening page of act 2.

No longer bound by any notion of "connecting" in the conventional sense it has for actors, my Wesley and Emma saw the dialogue as two separate compositions, playing contrapuntally, as an act 2 overture setting forth two motifs, the very distinct, but dissimilar mind-sets of the two children. Signaled by nothing more than a two-second fade from general stage lighting to that surreal monologue lighting discussed above, Emma's curiously sudden monologue now seemed right. The monologue was an extension for one character of what had been two monologues played simultaneously, parading as conversation but obviously not abiding by the normal rules of stage dialogue. Now, in the larger context of a play at once conventional and symbolic, real and surreal, the otherwise difficult dialogue became *natural, inevitable*. In the cinema, we could accomplish this with a split screen.

"I FEEL I'M AUDITIONING FOR THE FAMILY"

Depending on your perspective, it may be a truism or a piece of transparent flattery to say that directors can learn from actors. As I have suggested above, a complaint, a challenge, the urge to make a character as full as possible, curiosity about a specific moment in the play, all can serve the actor in developing a character and, in turn, teach the director about the very play on which he or she has labored alone for months while developing a concept. It was an actor's instinct, expressed as an offhand remark, that very much affected a production of Jules Feiffer's *Little Murders* that I directed a few seasons back.[3]

I had long wanted to do a "black comedy," and *Little Murders* is surely one of the best of this genre. Feiffer had also been *the* cartoonist of my college generation. With his neurotic characters, minimalist style, mordant commentary on our social foibles and obsessions, we saw him as on the very frontier of sophistication, the polar opposite from the cartoonists of "Dick Tracy" or "Dagwood."

At the center of the play is the Newquist family, headed by an early prototype for television's Archie Bunker, here the ironically named Carol Newquist. A male chauvinist pig, he chafes at his feminine first name. Carol is attended by his unliberated wife Marjorie, highly liberated daughter Patsy, and son Kenny, a closet homosexual. A dysfunctional family like Shepard's, but with an equal mixture of comedy and pseudotragedy, the Newquists struggle to adjust to Patsy's fiancée, the pacifist Alfred who riles her father with his theories of non-aggression. The "black" side of the comedy comes when Patsy is killed by a stray bullet as she embraces Alfred near the living room window. By act 3 Alfred, shocked by her untimely death, has become a bully and, accepted into the family as something of a "second son," joins them at the end, shooting strangers on the street below. Outside, New York City has been taken over by crooks. What is the nuclear family to do but board itself inside the house and, for amusement, take pot shots at people on the sidewalk? The Kitty Genovese case hovers over the play: that incident where a young girl was raped and murdered on a city street while hundreds of apartments dwellers, safe inside, looked on, with no one coming to her aid or even bothering to call the police. As a consequence, *Little Murders* navigates between that mordant humor of Feiffer and a protest against the model American family so celebrated in popular culture.

The Newquists, including Alfred, were relatively clear for us; it was the three visitors who presented the challenge. Feiffer spaces them carefully over the three acts: the Judge, an old friend of the family, who in act 1 comes to persuade the young couple to restore the name of God to their impending marriage ceremony; the Reverend Dupas in act 2, a hippie minister who sanctions every form of human behavior, from adultery to masturbation; and in the final act, Lieutenant Practice, investigating not only Patsy's murder but 345 other homicides, all remaining unsolved. Wonderful, long monologues, each is several pages of small type, but to me they seemed to have been "dropped in" by the playwright, comic cameos with only the most tangential relation to the Newquist story. "An excuse for three cartoon-like portraits," I muttered to myself.

I decided not to share this concern with my actors, and so it was something of a surprise when the actor who was to play the Judge remarked during our conversations after the read-through, "My monologue, in fact all three of them, looks like an audition piece to me." He had, I thought, confirmed my worst fears, but when I asked him if he meant what I feared, that the monologue bore only a meager relevance to the play, he replied, "No, I mean 'audition piece' in the sense that I feel I'm *auditioning* for the family." Urging him to say more, I got, "coming from the outside, trying to get in . . . get in with their—what would you call it?—world view, trying to influence the Newquists, to win them over, the way, you know, when I'm auditioning in real life I try to win over, sell myself to the director." I pushed him even further, but could get nothing more from him. After all, it was just his "feeling," one he had not yet articulated.

I decided to go with this feeling, to adopt his more optimistic metaphor of auditioning and to discard my own negative suspicions. After making a suggestion to each of the three that they treat their time on-stage as "the creation of a little world," or "a small play within the larger play," with my Stage Manager's help I reworked the rehearsal schedule so that until the final week I would rehearse separately with the Judge, Reverend Dupas, and Lieutenant Practice. That is, I would keep them away from the family, allowing the Newquists to bond among themselves, both as characters and as actors. This went against everything I usually do with rehearsals, for while I schedule scenes in order to make the most efficient use of my actors, and to respect their schedules, I generally spend the first two weeks doing in sequence smaller sections of the play, each section getting a block of rehearsal time, before running the play act by act near the end of the third week. With *Little Murders*, I would dismiss the rest of the cast and, alone with the "visitors" (as we now called them), rehearse the monologues by themselves at the end of the evening. Not until the final week would we integrate the visitors with the rest of the cast.

However, this presented no major technical problems. For the Judge's monologue, the simplest to block, Patsy and Alfred sat on the sofa, the mother on a nearby chair, while he played the entire stage. I cast a vivacious African-American actress as Dupas, a very cool, hip person in real life, to emphasize how radical she appears at this middle-class white wedding. After some initial mixing with the guests, she delivers her "sermon" to the seated guests. And while there was some tricky business with Lieutenant Practice's ordering Marjorie to get him cookies and milk (after she mistakenly brings him cheese) and then having another stray bullet from the street shatter the glass in his hand, he delivers his McCarthy-like tirade on conspiracy "from the right and left" (Feiffer 2002, 59) to a seated family, stunned by his harangue.

Their progress thus concealed from the rest of the cast, my three actors did indeed create little worlds, their own separate and wonderfully idiosyncratic mini-plays. The Judge quickly abandoned his object of convincing the lovers to restore God to the ceremony and, instead, defended his way of life, the old hard-work and suffering-is-good ethic that he fears is passé in the modern world. As he struggles to get back to the issue of God, we realize that his divinity is an object of both his adoration and despair: his God is so cruel that the Judge not so secretly wishes he were "dead." Dupas moved from the socially adept, new-age minister, eager to please every taste and to offend no one's lifestyle, to a raving evangelist of immorality, a parody of the 1960s protestors whose anarchism could be as much self-aggrandizement as genuine philosophy. Lieutenant Practice changed from the efficient detective to a not-so-subtle caricature of Joseph McCarthy, mad as a hoot owl, seeing conspirators (his personal Communists) everywhere, incredulous that no one else shares his fear that the 345 apparently random murders are part of a larger malignant plan tragically beyond human comprehension.

When the three visitors were at last integrated with the rest of the production, when they brought their characters back to their fellow actors, the results were everything a director could wish for.

All nine cast members, each in a very personal way, now saw a reason behind the visitors, their relation to the play's overall world. Indeed, we had to lengthen rehearsal time to accommodate the inevitable discussions that followed a night's scene work. A college professor when I

am not a director, I fell into the familiar role of teacher leading a class-
room discussion. I summarize their findings below.

The three visitors were fully developed, but isolated selves, only complete in their own little worlds: the past for the Judge, amorality for
Dupas, and a nightmare of conspiracies for Practice. Against these
static worlds is set that of the family, an evolving world where secrets
are exposed (Kenny's sexuality), bliss turns into sorrow (Patsy's murder), change occurs (the adoption of Alfred into the family), and dis-
cord leads to accord with the united family at the end happily shooting
at passersby, then sharing a meal together. To move from the Judge to
Practice is to move from questionable old-fashioned values to that assault on the nation's stability, not to mention sense of decency, posed by
the McCarthy era. Yet as the visitors become more extreme, the family
becomes more "normal," in a strange twisting of that word. For the
Newquists can at length only define themselves in opposition to everything outside their apartment. They are the "gated community" gone
mad. Now content within themselves, at peace, all differences resolved,
even Patsy's memory erased, they are exclusive, self-contained, not just
indifferent but actually hostile to the world that teems just outside. In
our production, the window looking out to the street was placed downstage, equidistant between the theater's two audience sections. The
house thereby became that outside world, and it was from there, at the
end, a photographer emerged to take a picture of the happy family. Put
even more directly, the family cannot exist in the outside world; they
are locked in this apartment forever. Such interaction as they have with
others will now be pretty much confined to Alfred's beating up people
on the street, whether or not there is provocation being of no consequence. That outside world, in Alfred's new aesthetics, has degenerated
from the portraits he once took, to commercial photographs where objects were more interesting to him than people, to dots. He now blows
up photos so that reality is microcosmically reformulated as the black
and gray dots, the atomistic but incomprehensible basis of the larger
picture. To take up my actor's revealing metaphor, the visitors "audition" for the family, but are rejected, are not cast.

The actors' reading, this product of the two casts, had a major influence on the production. For example, we used special lighting for the
three visitors' monologues. Further, all three actors were encouraged
to make those monologues very much set pieces, written beforehand,
"canned" in the sense of being pre-conceived, memorized. Monologues,
not dialogues, they involved no connecting with fellow actors. Clearly
the family's more natural acting style clashed with the visitors' formal,

rhetorical delivery. The audience actually became hostile to the visitors: Alfred rejects the judge with "You're not going to marry us" (Feiffer 2002, 33), so deflating him that he accuses the young man of being a "smart punk," then exits with almost a whimper: "He made me very late" (33). Dupas only manages to enrage the family and the wedding guests. At last they turn on him; my Fight Choreographer had a field day staging their gangland-styled assault on the minister. Practice exits accusing the family of being part of the conspiracy, ordering them not to leave town (59).

On Practice's exit, Carol, the Archie-Bunker husband, almost goes insane as he rages against "the rising tide" of crime, demanding security cameras "in every building lobby, in every elevator, in every apartment, in every room," or "lobotomies for anyone who earns less than ten thousand a year" (59–60). He then collapses onstage and is carried off by Alfred and Marjorie. The father "dies" in a sense, a victim of Practice's intrusion with his neurosis about crime. At length, the family starts to reconstitute itself. The weapon calling up the motto "a man's home is his castle," or the NRA's insane argument about our right to bear arms, the gun brings first Alfred and Kenny together, then Carol and Marjorie. *Little Murders* ends with a blissful and no less terrifying hymn to family unity. In Marjorie's closing words: "It's so nice to have my family together again. You know, for a while I was really worried" (63).

Reversing the normal practice, it was the actors' discoveries that greatly influenced the director's concept. They had replaced whatever I had devised before rehearsals began.

"WE ARE ALL THE CAPTAIN"

In August 1986, I was traveling on a liner down the coast of China with my family. I had just finished a month teaching Shakespeare and the modern playwrights at Jilin University and working with the Changchun Modern Drama Company on everything from Shakespeare's *The Merry Wives of Windsor* to Beckett's *Come and Go*. At midnight, unable to sleep, I wandered out alone on the deck. The coast of the People's Republic of China passed by, the darkness interrupted occasionally by a light on shore. For some reason, I was possessed with the idea of visiting the captain. On the top deck I found a large, circular room; inside five men were seated around a table, drinking tea, enjoying each other's company. I opened the door and asked, "Who's the captain?" They laughed politely, and then one replied, "We are *all* the captain." I was invited to join them, and soon it was explained to me that on some Chinese vessels there was no single captain. Rather, the ship was steered by a committee! All five were captains! They admitted that the arrangement made decisions difficult at times, but that they also liked this shared responsibility. "We are never lonely," one explained. I suspect the custom represented a blend of the ancient Chinese notion of placing the community over the individual with the Marxist avoidance of the "cult of personality."

Directing a production or, rather, being part of the company that stages a play is for me a lot like steering a boat by committee. Oh, there is a director, and the buck stops with him or her. But around that table, joining the director, sit the designers and the actors. The boat's voyage is a shared responsibility. Actors have, time and time again, taught me this is so.

3

Actors, the Set, and the Audience

ACTORS DO NOT WORK IN A VACUUM; NOR IS THEIR RELATIONSHIP with the director exclusive. In point of fact, their characters are shaped by many hands. Those hands include the designers and the audience. The former take suggestions from directors and actors: an adjustment to the set here, an addition to a costume there. But, just as often, designers can be "proactive," to use the politicians' term, initiating rather than just responding and, in this way, shaping the performance. The same holds true with the audience, especially an audience that the director and actors have tried to involve in the production. Audiences, I have found, are continually accepting, rejecting, adding to, qualifying, judging, playing with whatever happens onstage. And it would be the foolish actor or director who ignores their influence. I illustrate these general observations with accounts of productions of Brecht's *Galileo* and two plays by Pinter, *The Lover* and *Old Times*.

ISLANDS IN THE OCEAN

Galileo was the first play by Brecht that I directed and I was determined to meet the playwright and his theories about the theater more than halfway.[1] As he wished, the audience would be no mere passive body of spectators but, instead, involved in the onstage action, sharing the same space as the actors, not to mention illuminated by the same lighting rather than sitting anonymous in the darkness (See Brecht 1964, 20–22, 26–29, 33–42; Gray 1978, 67–89; Hecht 1960, 94–96; Needle and Thompson 1980, 120–39; Sokel 1989, 177–92).

I decided to play *Galileo* on three circular stages, each ten feet in diameter and raised nine inches from the floor, located on the upper-right, upper-left, and downside center of the large rectangular room of the Acrosstown Repertory Theatre. With these three stages resembling islands, the audience would surround them on all sides like an ocean.

Crosswalks painted on the floor connected the stages; an added cross-walk extending from the downstage to the double doors on the theater's east side led to the lobby. If, for example, an actor moved from stage 1 (upper right) onto the crosswalk to stage 2 (down side), he or she would thereby pass through spectators seated on either side. Conversely, the spectators would have to adjust their posture as the action moved from one stage to another. During rehearsals, we even learned to use these crosswalks as additional playing areas. Also, not being able to keep the stage light from spilling onto the surrounding chairs actually allowed us to satisfy Brecht's notion of the audience's being lit like the actors (Homan 1989, 78–105).

To blur the lines further between actors and audience, I decided that, rather than exiting backstage when a scene was finished, the actors would take a seat in the house, in one of two specially designated sections. There would be no offstage proper. The scene completed, the actor as character would become actor as fellow audience member, part of the "ocean" of spectators surrounding the three stages. The actors would now play two characters: one in Brecht's play, the other as spectator. Brecht himself speaks of the need for the actor's being at once in a role while also standing outside the character, thinking about this fictive person as he or she might exist in that real political/economic world outside the theatre (Sokel 1989, 177–92).

I even flirted with the idea of no designated section for actors, having the actors, instead, take any available seat. But given our full houses, and the need to have the actors sit towards the center to facilitate their taking the stage for the next scene, this idea was quickly abandoned.

Then an accident happened during rehearsals. At first thinking that Galileo, his teacher, has abandoned the *Discoursi* and thereby capitulated to the authorities, Andrea in scene 13 exits in high spirits when he learns of Galileo's plans to smuggle the manuscript across the border to a printer. One night I noticed that when our Andrea took his seat in the actor-A section, after saying a tearful farewell to his teacher, he was still too *high* from the emotions of the scene, was still in character. On the spot, I asked my Galileo to deliver his lines, "I gave him his first lesson; when he held out his hand, I had to remind myself that he is teaching now" (Brecht 1966, 125), not to Virginia as the script indicates but to the former Andrea now seated with the audience. The effect was *electric*, for in a production designed to bring actor and audience closer, whatever barrier remained was now erased. When Galileo returned to the world onstage with his question to Virginia, "How is the sky tonight?" that world was reasserted yet also qualified since our Andrea in the audience now looked on with his fellow spectators as Virginia mimed opening the shutters. When she replied, simply, "Bright," Andrea showed his pleasure as a spectator. His subtext would go something like: "The night is indeed bright since my teacher has taught me by his own savage self-assessment and this decision about the manuscript the most important of all lessons." His response would itself be reflected by that of the real-life audience surrounding him. We even learned how to intensify this effect by having some of the actors seated nearby push Andrea's chair a little forward as he exited the stage, so that everyone in the audience would have a clear view of this man both in and out of character. For most of the play our lighting was otherwise fairly neutral: no gels, no colors, with the lighting limited to following the action as it moved from one stage, through a crosswalk, to another stage. However, I made a rare exception for this one moment. As Virginia pronounced "Bright," we raised the stage illumination about thirty percent.

This discovery that the actor, while seated with the audience, could also continue in character led to numerous other erasures of the distinction between the stage and the house. At the end of scene 10, for example, once Galileo and Virginia heard the stern words of the Lord Chamberlain, "that the Florentine court [was] no longer in a position to oppose the request of the Holy Inquisition to interrogate [Galileo] in Rome" (107), Galileo slumped to a seat just offstage in the actor-B section, head in hands. A beaten, humiliated old man, he was comforted by Virginia who, sitting next to her father, clung to him, cradling him like a mother. The two actors held this position throughout the next scene, leaving their seats only at the end so that our Galileo could exit out the double doors in order to come back through when he gave his recantation in scene 12.

Or, at the end of scene 13 after Virginia's "Bright," our Galileo, like a stagehand, removed his chair from the stage, placing it in a space between the chairs of two spectators sitting on the upside of stage 1. There, still in character, he watched with them the final scene where Andrea smuggled the *Discoursi* over the border.

During one rehearsal, after the First Senator had, as planned, offered her a seat to his right in the actor-A section, Virginia by mistake took an empty seat to his left, right beside Ludovico. Later in the rehearsal, Ludovico came to me and proposed the following bit of stage business: the Senator offers the seat to his right; Virginia, however, sees the handsome Ludovico two seats to his left and in mime boldly asks the Senator if she might instead sit near the young man. An old married man not realizing her motive, the Senator inadvertently brings the young couple together. As Galileo onstage talked to Mr. Matti about his iron factory, Virginia and her newfound companion engaged in some silent flirtatious conversation, thereby establishing a courtship, however hurried or accidental. Yet, torn between Ludovico and her father, Virginia impulsively tried to unite them with her line, "Here's Ludovico to congratulate you father" (58), delivered not onstage but from the audience.

Even as this decision to have actors double as audience members reinforced Brecht's notion of the audience as an equal partner in the production, it also led to our finding parallels in the play itself: those instances in *Galileo* where characters onstage function as an audience. In the opening scene, for example, Andrea watches Galileo sarcastically describe the "map of the sky according to the wise men of ancient Greece" (47). When Andrea crossed from our stage 1 to stage 2, joining his teacher there, seduced by him after his initial protest ("You're off again, Mr. Galilei" [49]), I had Mrs. Sarti stand in Andrea's former place, like an audience watching Galileo demonstrate the new cosmos. Likewise, the would-be student Ludovico, entering stage 1, looked first at the ancient map, and then for a few seconds at Galileo and Andrea on stage 2, before coughing politely to catch Galileo's attention. The Curator on stage 1 saw Galileo, to whom he had just given money, rush back to stage 2 to toss the measurements for an optical tube to Andrea, who from near the double doors had in turn watched Galileo greet this second unexpected visitor. Or in scene 6 Virginia and the Inquisitor, on stage 3, watched an embarrassed, angry Galileo trudge behind the two Cardinals as they crossed to the actor-A section. In this fashion, Brecht's text sustained the discoveries that the set suggested to the actors.

THE SET DESIGNER AND RICHARD'S "YOU LOVELY WHORE"

My Set Designer for *The Lover* led the way here.[2] He asked me, "How's Richard's last line going to sound in the 1990s? You know, what with women's lib and all that?" The line in question is Richard's "You lovely whore"(Pinter 1965, 26), an apparent instance of the politically incorrect if there ever was one. I could only say to my designer that I would try to make the production justify Richard's portrait of Sarah, so that his words would be loving and proper rather than derogatory.

What I discovered with the actors is that both husband and wife need to see each other as a mixture of lust and wit, appetite and intellect, body and soul. Their role-playing, pretending to be each other's lovers, is only a stop-gap measure; reality in this work by a playwright sometimes accused of sacrificing meaning to snappy dialogue is the end. "Wholeness" would be the operative term from our own self-help groups. My general request to the designer was to give me a set that was simultaneously "real" and "playful," reflecting the play's division between the real-life human problems of marriage and that game playing to which the couple has turned for a solution.

His "real" part consisted of a divan stage right, a small bar to its right where Sarah prepares their evening drinks, a sofa halfway downstage-center, a round table with overhanging lace cover upstage-left, and "Richard's chair" downstage-left. Behind the sofa were bookcases, the pristine volumes never having been read, there only for show. An orderly room, not especially inspiring, nothing in it to show any individual taste, the type or room that, when entering, we would pronounce as "lovely" but without conviction. This was the "real" half of the split set.

The "unreal" or theatrical half was the floor. With squares of rich inlaid wood, their size exaggerated downstage and diminished upstage to give the sharp perspective of depth that one might encounter in a Renaissance painting of a palace room, the stage looked like a huge chess board, a game board. The chess squares thereby reinforced the pervasive theatricality in the marriage. In fact, during the opening encounter with Max, where he plays a stranger picking up Delores in the park, both actors moved mechanically on those squares like exaggerated chess pieces, "like children playing hopscotch on chalk-lined squares in the street," as a crew member observed.

Pinter himself was responsible for the other theatrical touch in the set. *The Lover* was originally a television play, and the numerous costume changes present, of course, no problem in that medium: one simply stops the taping process before starting a new scene. In live theater, however, his television play presented problems: there was too much empty time when Richard and Sarah had to change from morning to evening outfits or from evening to bedtime wear, not to mention the changes to and from Max and Delores. Our solution was to construct a "changing area" upstage-left, its walls those thick blocks of glass about the size of cinder blocks through which the onlooker can see only a blurred image of someone on the other side. We did all our changes there, rather than backstage. It was very discreet for all the audience saw were indistinct forms and splashes of color as, say, Sarah took off her modest morning dress and got into her Delores outfit, or Richard changed from his business suit to come out as Max: tight-fitting pants, sports shirt open to reveal a hairy chest, fashionable captain's jacket, gold chain around his neck. In this play about role-playing, where the couple has both used and then abused the theater in an attempt to save their marriage, the audience could watch the costume changes. At very least the audience had something to do during the changes, for a standard rule in theater is never to leave the stage empty for too long: losing their focus, treating the empty space as if it were an intermission, the audience invariably falls to talking.

Music from the album *Ella Fitzgerald Sings Cole Porter* accompanied these onstage costume changes, the longest of which took thirty seconds. Besides entertaining those in the house and establishing the sophisticated mood of this love comedy, we also used the music to reflect on or anticipate scenes. For example, Porter's "Night and Day" played between the opening morning scene and Richard's return at evening in scene 2. "In the Still of the Night" faded into the romantic scene where Richard and Sarah, his arms around her waist, look out at the moon from their balcony. During the fade before the scene where Max rejects Delores, we heard "Just One of Those Things."

"You lovely whore" at last took on a double-meaning that did not violate political correctness; in its way the dual set sustained this fact. By the end of the play Richard *is* being playful. He views his wife now as a partner, his equal, surely not his inferior, let alone whore. In fact, for him Sarah is the very woman she herself had described earlier when, trying to humiliate him about his "whore," she reminds Richard, "You have such taste. You care so much for grace and elegance in women." This prompts the husband to add, "And wit" (Pinter 1987, 10). She is indeed "lovely," and in calling her "whore" he is both playful, ironic, yet serious in the sense that, now with Max gone, having abandoned game-playing, their private theater, he is able to delight in her physical person, and in his as well. As the lights fell, our Richard and Sarah were locked in an amorous, *very* amorous embrace. In the darkness, just seconds before the lights went back up for curtain calls, the audience heard the first sounds of foreplay.

PINTER'S FURNITURE

I have discussed earlier the tension in Pinter's *Old Times* between the seemingly light dialogue and the serious issues just below the surface: the characters' recreations of the past, the possibility that Kate is, all along, a playwright directing the encounter between her two rivals. No less, the set, for which the playwright provides very specific directions, reinforces this tension.[3]

Pinter asks for a sparse set. The sitting room of act 1 has two sofas and an armchair; for the bedroom of act 2, two divans and a chair. In both acts there is a window upstage. However, the simple set is complicated by his asking that the arrangement of the furniture in the second act duplicate that of act 1 but "in reversed position"(Pinter 1971, 1). That is, we move from sitting room to bedroom and yet we do not move at all: the act 2 set is the (reverse) mirror image of act 1. Again, *Old Times* goes from the sitting room, an appropriate place in which to entertain a guest, to the bedroom, a most inappropriate place by normal social etiquette. We might see act 2 as a repetition of act 1 with its own variation, the "child" of the previous act where Kate has shown signs of acquiring her own identity. At the end of act 1 Kate turns down Anna's offer to draw her bath. And in the second act, the taciturn Kate of act 1 gives way to a confident woman, defining her new self as she enters the bedroom refreshed from that bath and, at the end, delivering the play's longest and most complex speech to a silent audience of two onstage.

While he describes the home as a converted farmhouse, Pinter does not specify the style of its furniture, although Deeley does speak of the divans in act 2 as having castors and hence as mobile so that they can be arranged at various angles to each other. Nor does Pinter dictate the exact arrangement for the furniture in act 1, although whatever arrangement the set designer with the director's advice chooses determines that of act 2, but again, "in reverse position."

Given the motif of triangles and the tension between dualities (Deeley/Anna, Anna/Kate, past/present, London/present location), I placed the two sofas at a forty-five degree angle to each other, two-thirds of the way upstage. Downstage-center, forming the triangle's apex, was a drum table. In act 2 the two divans occupied precisely the same space occupied earlier by the sofas. And there was a touch of unreality, the mysterious: the drum table reappeared in act 2. I had borrowed the idea from the early television series *Love American Style*, where each week, whatever the story or its setting, there appeared at some point an ornate brass bed, symbol of eternal lovemaking.

Though sparse, the set was suggestive in its arrangement. Most certainly it is not a cluttered set like that required by, say, Pinter's *The Homecoming*. And while I wanted all the focus to be on the three characters and the dialogue, the set would be something other than a "playing area." That it was so minimal would surely lead the audience, their threshold for details lowered, to focus on what *was* there.

For me, the set reflected both the sterility, the dryness of this marriage and, at the same time, the lush, seductive past of Kate's London days. Therefore, for act 1 the two sofas, both two-seaters thereby contributing to the "odd man out" motif, were nondescript and conventional. No less unremarkable was Deeley's armchair on stage left. However, this generic furniture rested on a complex, multicolored Persian rug. Downstage was that ornate drum table, a stunning piece, an antique of nineteenth-century design with tripod feet and brass inlays around the edges. On Kate's half of the table were three delicate tea cups and saucers. On Deeley's half, a bulky decanter of brandy, a gaudy piece of crystal accompanied by three oversized snifters. That drum table served as a "safe place" where characters could escape when the competition for Kate became too oppressive.

The divans for act 2 were longish, functional benches, yet across each was thrown a single large pillow, deep reddish purple in color. To compensate, the Persian rug was removed for act 2, exposing a rather ordinary carpet.

Upstage was a long, floor-to-ceiling window covered by porous drapes. Here is where Anna stands at the start of the play, invisible to Kate and Deeley. For act 1, along with the general stage lighting, two amber spots behind the window shined through those porous drapes. Blue gels were substituted during the intermission, so that, in contrast to the warm atmosphere, the mood in act 2 was colder, as if the first act's superficial conviviality had given way to the sterile bedroom to which the evening's entertainment has inexplicably moved.

In general, neither room gave any clue about its inhabitants; no pictures on the walls, no object of art, family heirlooms, furniture, or accessories that would indicate something of the owner's taste. Perhaps the sterile bedroom bathed in cold blue gels even confirmed Anna's hope that the marriage was ripe for exploitation. In the final moments, even the bedroom dissolved as the light focused on Kate, her two competitors immobile, "dead" in semi-darkness on their respective divans. The house itself had been an illusion. My reading, as suggested earlier, was that all along the evening, the past, and the present, were part of Kate's dream. A surrogate for the playwright, she alone has been real. Pinter's stage direction at the end nicely came to the aid of this interpretation. The lights suddenly come up "full sharply. Very bright" (75). We held them for two seconds; the effect was that of a photographer's flash. *Old Times* had been a snapshot of Kate. Having created Deeley and Anna, or invoked them, she was the play's single character, its "star." The photograph now documented this fact.

SETS SPEAK

Sets speak. This is clear. Sometimes they speak too loudly. I recall productions where the set has swallowed up the actor, the designer surely not communicating with the director. Cecil Barton's elaborate black-and-white Ascot Downs set for *My Fair Lady* was so stunning that the audience invariably applauded, for two minutes on one occasion, forcing the actors to freeze. They too were clad in black and white outfits, and in that frozen position blended in with Barton's set.

Some playwrights call for very little. *Waiting for Godot* asks only for a rock and one leafless tree, usually located somewhere far upstage, the perfect minimalist image for this meeting place where the lead character fails to appear. Beckett does call for a few scrawny leaves to grow on that tree for the second act. During a prison production of that play with which I was involved, the inmates, not being allowed to leave for intermission and with their expectations sharpened by Beckett's sparse set, always reacted loudly when the stagehand came on with five leaves to paste on the tree (Homan 1979, 122–29). In Beckett's *Breath* the set is the entire play. With the lights coming up on a five-second cue, we see a stage strewn with rubbish, "no verticals, all scattered and lying," to the accompaniment of a "cry," an "inspiration of recorded vagitus." Then the lights hold for a second five seconds on the stage tableau, followed by a final five-second cue for the fade, accompanied by a "cry" and "expiration" (Beckett 1974, 89). No actors, no dialogue, just a set with lights and sound, but one that, for this playwright, embodies the entire human cycle, from womb to tomb.

Sam Shepard's sets, in contrast, are full-blown, a presence often as significant as the actors. In *Curse of the Starving Class* the four principal characters go to the refrigerator numerous times, finding it empty, filling it with food, looking for food, shutting the door carefully as well as carelessly, and, at the end, tearing food out ravenously. Their attitude toward that refrigerator becomes part of the dialogue. And, in the final moments, the stage strewn with food offers a graphic image of the dysfunctional family. As the thug Slater says, looking at the mess, "I couldn't live like this if you paid me" (Shepard 1981, 64). In a production of Shepard's *True West*, we had to take precautions not to injure the audience as Lee hacks away at the typewriter with a golf club, or later hurls onto the stage the toasters his brother Austin has stolen.[4] Trying to find a pencil, the frustrated writer tore into the kitchen cabinets, scattering corn flakes, among other breakfast items, all over the floor. As with *Curse*, the very condition of the stage speaks to this portrait of Shepard's Cain and Abel, these feuding brothers trying to meld one's real-life experience with the other's facility with words in order to write a successful script.

The set is there, with a permanence that dialogue cannot have. And audiences need to see the set. In Peter Shaffer's 1965 play *Black Comedy* the lights fail during a cocktail party within minutes of the opening of the first act, the guests stumbling about in the darkness, the evening ruined. However, now uninhibited by their not being seen, the characters reveal more about themselves than they would under the normal social conventions of a cocktail party. Only near the end of the second act are the lights restored. The director's first inclination was to play it for real, that is, with most of the two-hour play performed in darkness, almost like a radio drama. But try-out audiences objected: they wanted to *see* the set, not to mention the actors. Shaffer's simple solution was to open the play in total darkness, with the actors themselves pretending the lights are "on." In a program note the audience was asked to pretend that a dark stage was a fully lighted living room, and then, when the lights fail in their world, that a lit stage was one totally dark, for the characters. Accepting the convention the way, say, Shakespeare's audience accepted an aside, the audience, their sight restored, were perfectly content.

I have especially enjoyed working with those set designers who, abiding by the general concept I outline for them, go on to provide me with additional challenges, even opportunities: furniture placement that opens up all sorts of new options for blocking, a clever use of stage technology such as a revolving set, an object in the set that can serve multiple functions and thus solves a problem of logistics.

Some years ago my colleague John Cech asked if I would direct his stage adaptation of Marjorie Kinnan Rawlings's short story "The Secret River."[5] In this story, the author's own Cross Creek, Florida, is suffering since the fishing industry has dried up. Now worries over money are threatening marriages, the town itself mired in a deep depression. But a little girl hears of an old woman in the forest who knows the location of a secret river, a realm of the imagination where wishes come true. Advised by the old woman, she sets off with her dog to find this magical river and, after some close encounters with wild animals, comes upon the place. There, casting her line she pulls in hundreds of fish, brings them back to the village, feeds her neighbors, and, by her example of determination and concern for the town, restores the adults' faith, restores, as my colleague Cech would say, the "child within the adult." The town returns to prosperity.

I found Cech's adaptation a blend of that realism of which a regional writer like Rawlings is the master and a fantasy tale that was somewhat rare for her. The forest and the secret river are like a projection of the young child's imagination. Somehow a solid set, not to mention a realistic forest, seemed wrong for this blend. By good chance, I had been working with a wonderful choreographer, Jill Sonke-Henderson, and, while meeting with her on other matters, we hit upon the idea of using dancers as the set. That is, the Cross Creek residents in period costumes would share the stage with dancers in black leotards who would "become" the set: tables, chairs, the farmhouse interior, the upstage houses of the town, as well as the trees in the forest, the river, even the fish that the little girl catches. If an actor crossed to sit at the table, for example, a dancer would fly across stage to form a chair just in time; another dancer became a hat rack as the father, about to leave for work, stopped by the door for his cap. As the forest got thicker, the dancers suggested this through an ensemble movement, their arms entangled, enveloping the little girl as she moved about the stage in her search for the river. A graceful leap out of the river by a dancer stood for the little girl's pulling a fish onto the shore. All this to a full-length score by a gifted young guitarist.

The set for *The Secret River* spoke through very animate "objects." Indeed, there was nothing inanimate on the stage. Only humans. What is next? Holographic sets? Computer-generated scenery?

4

The Actor and the Prop: The Tape Recorder in Beckett's *Krapp's Last Tape*

FOR SOME THEATERGOERS, BECKETT IS DIFFICULT, ARCANE, TOO IN-
tellectual, inaccessible to the average audience. Such has not been my
experience, and I say this having done a tour of *Waiting for Godot* in the
Florida prison system before inmates, the majority of whom had little
schooling or little experience with the theater. Yet these inmates were
overwhelmed by this play about men waiting. Our first performance was
at Raiford, a maximum-security facility in Starke, Florida, where the
state houses its "lifers." As they had done twenty years before when the
Actor's Workshop staged *Godot* at San Quentin, the inmates continually
broke into the performance, addressing the characters, asking Vladimir
or Estragon what he meant when he said this, why Pozzo treated Lucky
so cruelly, or insisting the characters come downstage to "explain"
themselves. *Godot* had cut too close to their own lives; far from being a
disruptive audience, they were trying to be part of the evening, to collaborate with us (Homan 1979, 122–29). Besides talking with the actors
during the performance, they demanded to speak with us after the
show. Before a shocked warden, eager to get the men back into their
cells for the evening bed-check, and before no less shocked actors, the
inmates "wanted to talk about this Godot fellow. You know, the guy
who doesn't show. We've got some damn good ideas about who he
might be." Each inmate saw Godot in terms of his own needs, his own
feelings about waiting; each fashioned a personal interpretation.

Our experience at Raiford was later replicated nine times when,
under a grant from the Florida Humanities Council, we staged the play
in minimum- to maximum-security prisons, before audiences of men
and of women.[1] Clearly, Beckett was not inaccessible to the inmates.

For me this playwright is not dry or sterile or depressing. From very
different perspectives, two recent books on Beckett have suggested that
among the reasons his works engage us is his sense of visual presence.

Beckett elevates "the visual image over narrative story" (Essif 2002, 67); his work is structured like a piece of music, but instead of "ringing the changes on musical phrases, he does the same thing with shapes and patterns—of the stage space and movement within it, of gesture and the spoken word." At the heart of Beckett are "concrete, physical stage idioms" (Bradby 2001, 211–12). No matter how meager his physical stage, what is there communicates to the audience at a nonverbal, sensory, immediate level, and is compelling: the tree or rock in *Godot*, Winnie's mound or the revolver in *Happy Days*, cubes in *Act Without Words I* and *II*, the table and two chairs in *Ohio Impromptu*, a rocking chair, a mouth suspended upstage in *Not I*, the stuffed dog with three legs that is Hamm's companion in *Endgame*. With their voice-overs and meager dialogue, his five television plays push this visual dimension to the limit.

In *Krapp's Last Tape* there are spools of past recordings, a banana, a watch, an envelope, a dictionary, bottles, but, most prominent of all, is the tape recorder on the desk. Technically, that recorder is a prop, although it also functions as something of a miniature stage with its own recorded drama, as Krapp in his old age hunches over the machine listening to himself in his thirties talk about his life a decade before. In Beckett's minimalist theater that tape recorder stands out, intrudes, is omnipresent. It is a prop with a rich, complex function, reminding us not only of just how visual Beckett's plays are but of how central a prop can be in theatrical production.

I have both played the single character in *Krapp's Last Tape* and directed him, and so I speak here from a double perspective.[2] Beckett may be an acquired taste as, say, Neil Simon is not. Still, I have always found *Krapp's Last Tape* to be one of the most engaging, moving, human pieces for the stage, a threnody of despair and hope, a deeply felt statement about those things common to us all: the need to love and be loved, the fear of isolation, of growing old, the wish to lead our life over again, the dubious pleasure we take in withdrawing from the world and living within ourselves, those moments when we see ourselves clearly and painfully.

What Beckett Tells Us

Directors and actors sometimes complain that Beckett is "bossy" and prescriptive in his instruction, a bit like Shaw with his lengthy psychological descriptions of the characters or his sermonizing about the social values of his work. Actors complain that Vladimir and Estragon seem to float free of the past, have no clear histories on which an actor can pin a subtext. They complain that Krapp's listening to himself on the tape recorder leaves little to the actor's imagination. "I've got nothing more to do than deliver the lines," one actor told me. And far be it for the director or a designer to attempt to apply a concept to *Krapp's Last Tape*. It's all spelled out for them: the desk center stage, its drawers facing downstage, a tape recorder and boxes of tapes covering the top, with bright white lighting confined to the immediate area of the desk, the rest of the stage dark, Krapp himself dressed in a generic vaudevillian's outfit similar to that worn by the playwright's other lonely men in little rooms. Beckett even specifies that the voice is to be "cracked" and yet with "distinctive intonation" (Beckett 1959, 10); every bit of blocking, every gesture is indicated in the italicized entries in the text. When Krapp crosses the stage with the banana in his mouth, he is to appear "meditatively eating banana," executing "not more than four or five paces either way" (11).

Attitude, I believe, is everything here. What one might see as an overly prescriptive playwright, I prefer to think of as someone with enormous integrity, sure of what he wants, with the caveat that the play can be both what the playwright wants and more. From this perspective, the restrictions ultimately represent Beckett's own careful fulfilling of his half of the contract. To the other half the actor will bring his life experiences with old men, his own feelings about those daily journeys we all make into our past.

The director might interpret the specifics of set, costume, lighting, and movement as the interior world of the brain, Beckett's own "third" or "dark world" (Beckett 1957, 111–13). Like the set in *Endgame* with its two vertical eye-like upstage windows, the desk in *Krapp's Last Tape* may be the inside of Krapp's skull, its drawers the compartments of the brain or regions of the memory. The basic set suggests the idiosyncratic realm of the self whose isolation from the larger world is at once satisfying and terrifying in its loneliness.

Krapp's several exits backstage, to fetch a dictionary, more often to drink, signal those increasingly rare moments when he moves outside of this interior region. His room, a table, and "immediately adjacent area in strong white light" with the "rest of stage in darkness" (Beckett 1959, 10) may suggest that room/womb/tomb we find elsewhere in Beckett: the urns holding the characters in *Play*; the bench in *Come and Go*, lit from above and also surrounded by darkness; the imaginary spaces of the radio plays like *All That Fall*, *Embers*, *Cascando*, and *Words and Music* defined only by language; the single rooms of *Film*, *Eh Joe*, and *Ghost Trio*, whose lone proprietors go through an elaborate mime of shutting the door to the outside world. For the director, then, *Krapp's Last Tape* provides a challenge: under such restrictions, with the most minimal of sets, confined to a single character, with more than half the dialogue recorded, how can one respond to this solitary character, to this representative of the self, the buried world in all of us?

With *Krapp's Last Tape* I have tried to do just that, as both actor and director. I found it useful to divide the work into eleven sections or, given Beckett's affinity with composers and music, "movements." Below, I give them titles which at once define the texture and structure of a particular movement.

The Mime (9–12)

My Krapp was very old, arthritic even beyond the "laborious walk" of the stage direction, a man so unsure of his footing that his movements were graceless. Getting about irritated him, stood as a badge of his decay, of the wasted physical life he later calculates under "statistics" (16). For me, his "narrow trousers too short for him," "grimy white shirt," and "dirty white boots" (9) represented not just neglect but a purposeful defiance of order and fashion, the self-anger that he tries to pass off as contempt for the physical world.

The cluttered desk, however, is his sacred territory, a countersign to his pessimism, a stage on which are arrayed the boxes recording his life, his artistic output that mitigates the disorder of his past and its apparent lack of meaning, let alone progress. Cluttered from our view, to Krapp the desk appears very orderly, organized; all things are in their place, but the key is known only to him. The tapes are a still point, time frozen, and so when he "looks at watch" (10) he is reminded painfully of time, specifically of the appointment he has made with himself this evening to try his hand once again at creation by breaking a thirty-year silence and making a new recording. The outline for that recording is on that envelope he "takes out" of his pocket and then "puts back." Similarly, the tape he removes from the first drawer, peers at, and then locks back in the drawer is the new reel he intends to use.

As much as Krapp wants to attempt a creative act, he is afraid and therefore avoids this moment: to create is to expose oneself. To face an audience of one. The whole bit with the banana—stroking it, peeling it, dropping the skin at his feet, putting the end in his mouth, throwing the skin to the stage—he recognizes all too clearly as what psychologists would call an "avoidance reaction." Failing to distract him as much as the first time, the mime with the second banana is that much less satisfying. It is an irony that he puts the banana in the same pocket containing the envelope. Krapp never fools himself: he is painfully aware both of what he must do this evening and of how eager he is to avoid doing it.

This tension between desire and avoidance too great for Krapp to endure, he charges offstage, eager to escape the light. We hear him chugging a full bottle of wine. When he reappears, he holds a ledger. Another diversion. Defensively, Krapp thinks, "I'm not avoiding the new tape; I'm just listening to these old ones as a way of preparing myself. That's why I need the ledger: to make sure I get the right one." He suffers from "writer's block," although Krapp has no interest in publication as normally understood. Wiping his mouth, bringing his hands "smartly together" (12) gives the appearance of getting down to work.

FINDING THE SPOOL (12–13)

Krapp is always conscious of his weakness for self-deception. As he searches for the right entry in the ledger, and then the right spool, he tries to hoodwink himself and us. It is as if we were his conscience, an inner voice that cannot be denied. In the television play *Eh Joe* that voice is literal: the woman who speaks off-camera berating the solitary male on-camera, Joe, in his sleazy bedroom. As I played it, the entry Krapp seeks ("Farewell to love") is underlined in the ledger, spool five containing the episode with the woman on the boat, so clearly marked that Krapp, if he wanted, could find it easily, without thumbing through other spools. He recites the numbers of the spools, announcing the entries in the ledger: "Mother at rest at last," "the black ball," "the dark nurse," "slight improvement in bowel condition, "Memorable Equinox" (13). His stalling is half-hearted and bound to fail. He pretends to review more tapes so as to prepare himself, but there is only one entry that really interests him. As he has every night for the past thirty years, he cannot refrain from hearing again "Farewell to love," the episode with the woman on the boat, the one moment in his life when he was close to another human being. He relishes this moment, and yet becomes distraught because it contradicts the spuriously comforting routine of boredom and loneliness. Even Krapp laughs at his turning the page to read the final word in the entry "Farewell to love": he has long since memorized the entry, knows that "love" is on the back side of the page.

LISTENING (13–17)

Krapp, "assum [ing] listening posture" (13) before the tape recorder, becomes an audience located upstage of the table, mirroring the audience in the house. The tape recorder is the "stage" separating them. I like to remind actors that every monologue is really a dialogue, that the character is always talking to an audience of himself or herself.

Krapp's physical responses and sounds constitute a second text, his dialogue with the voice on the tape. He "lean[s] forward," "set[s] himself more comfortably," "closes his eyes briefly," "broods," and twice joins in a "brief laugh" with the voice on the machine. That second text will be augmented, of course, by whatever responses, gestures, and movement are added by the actor. Beyond this, since the voice on the machine, Krapp at thirty-nine, is reflecting on his life over the previous ten years, he stands apart, looking at himself at an earlier age.

While "settling himself more comfortably," he knocks the boxes off the table and, cursing at the accident, switches off the tape recorder and "sweeps boxes and ledger violently to the ground." The physical actions underscore the fact that this is no mere radio broadcast with a passive listener. I chose to make Krapp's response to the accident a comic, yet pathetic instance of his wanting to blame fate, the gods, anything outside himself for whatever happens. He was just getting comfortable, surely didn't mean to knock the box off the table; the act was probably inevitable given his arthritic condition.

Until the midpoint of this movement, where he closes his eyes briefly, Krapp hurls himself back and forth between guarded optimism and raw pessimism. He is "sound as a bell" yet plagued by some "old weakness." There is a "new light" above his table, which he admits is a "great improvement," yet while this makes him "feel less alone" in "all this darkness," the change is only "in a way," the relief is only partial. Krapp struggles here, like some crabby, geriatric Tantalus, each affirmative statement begetting its opposite.

Beckett, it has been observed, has an instinctive grasp of the medium (Reid 1968, 219–21). In fact, the stimulus for the present play was a tape recorder sent him by the BBC so that he could listen to his radio plays that had been broadcast over the station's third channel. Beckett had never operated a tape recorder before, never owned one, yet here he cuts to the essence of the medium, elevates the machine itself to an aesthetic statement: the tape recorder as an extension of the listener, bringing the past (when the tape was made) into the present (the act of listening). This conflation of past and present is even more pronounced in this movement's second half, signaled by the voice wanting to "close my eyes and try and imagine . . . those things worth having when all the dust has . . . settled." The recorded voice is matched by action as the live actor "closes his eyes briefly."

As if refreshed by this otherwise painful act of listening to that cynical self caught between affirmation and negation, Krapp moves from his little room, out from the self. Although only implied on the tape, his landscape expands. He hears Miss McGlome singing, calls her a "wonderful woman," and speculates what she must have been like as a girl. He digs up memories of a Bianca on Kedar Street, with whom he had a fleeting romance; despite his sarcasm, he credits her with "incomparable" eyes. This verbal geography is matched by his being even more active here, using the pauses in the recording to reflect on what he hears, even switching off the tape at one point to "brood" before switching back on, and twice joining in the laughter on tape, as well as twice laughing on his own at the recording.

Having interacted more fully with the voice, Krapp for the first time approaches the most painful subject so far, his failed literary career. This in turn reminds him of a prop. The "envelope" with a "few notes" mentioned earlier on the tape and buried in the desk for thirty years is the same one now resting in his pocket, a reminder that he has things to do tonight, Frost-like "promises to keep." Krapp can take no more. This movement closes with his switching off the tape in the middle of the sentence "When I look —."

INTERLUDE (17)

This short movement has the feel of an intermission. After "brood"ing, trying to recover from his evasions and procrastinating, after the painful experience of hearing his youthful self Krapp goes offstage, taking solace in drink by draining three bottles. Though its lyrics are hackneyed, the prophetic song he sings offstage, "Now the day is over," proves too much for him. There is no escape; the intermission is over quickly and he comes back into the light, resuming the listening posture.

"VIDUITY" (18)

Now Krapp's interaction with the tape recorder intensifies. The passage he had aborted before intermission is played again in full: the account of his mother's death, in "the late autumn" in the "house on the canal where [she] lay a-dying." For all his cynicism, here Krapp exposes to himself and his audience a vulnerable, sensitive side. As Krapp, I saw myself as a young boy, my mother vibrant, wearing a long skirt, playing with me, and then our going to the window to watch boats pass down the canal, her arms around me, my head resting on her breast, a reassuring glow from the fireplace. Outside it was cold, with that uncertain twilight of those autumnal months serving as a transition to winter. The picture was something a French impressionist might paint, the ambers and rich browns of the room dissolving into the gray, laced with black from the outside.

Overwhelmed by the vivid picture of childhood, Krapp switches off the tape recorder, but not before becoming distracted by the word "viduity." I left the desk, going backstage to find the dictionary. In point of fact, Krapp knows the word's defintion, but uses the mere act of getting up to fetch the dictionary as a distraction. The word's double meaning sets the boundaries of the physical world: "viduity" refers at once to sterility (the "state—or condition of being—or remaining—a widow—or widower") and fecundity, the bird's black plumage used to attract females. He smiles, refreshed by this linguistic surprise.

APPROACHING THE DESIRED PASSAGE (19–22)

When Krapp resumes, the passage on the tape is the longest played so far. As he sits by the bench, staring up at his mother's window, wishing she were dead, a "dark young beauty" pushing a perambulator comes by; when he ventures to speak to her, she threatens to call the police. Despite the woman's attitude, the narrator remembers her eyes being like "chrysolite." Krapp switches off and "broods." When he switches on the recorder, the story concludes with two interwoven pictures: the blinds being drawn on the window to his mother's room, sign of her death, and at his feet a dog, indifferent to the death, begging him to toss a ball. With a human, almost comic touch, the narrator decides to give the ball to the dog instead of keeping it. The physical ball gone, its essence remains: "I shall feel it, in my hand, until my dying day." Separated from his early self, Krapp now draws closer to the tape recorder.

In the movement's second half he has a true Joycean "epiphany." Standing on the end of the jetty one night in March, in the howling wind, brooding on his mother's death, and on the death of his artistic talent, the foam flying against the granite rocks, the wind gauge spinning, the dark illumined only by the lighthouse, he realized that his whole life has been spent trying to conceal "the darkness in [himself]." For me, as actor and director, Krapp in a moment of Hamlet-like introspection sees his tragedy not as imposed but as born of his own self-deceit, his unwillingness to confront this darkness, his own malignancy. Krapp switches off and on the recording three times: he doesn't want to, even as he knows he cannot help but listen to this exquisitely profound revelation.

When he winds the tape forward, he is once more frustrated: the voice is still trying to describe the revelation, to clothe the epiphany in words. He hears "understands" but then, cursing, stops the tape on the phrase "the fire —," to be completed only at the end of the play as "the fire within me."

Again he switches off, then on, winding the tape too far this time, for now he picks up the final few sentences of the passage he has been seeking all night, the account of the woman in the boat, the "farewell to love." It stands out against all the darkness of his life, against old age and sterility, and accumulated cynicism. It is a passage of incredible beauty, a concrete poetry bursting with implications. The camera-like close-up of the lovers, his "face in her breast, and [his] hand on her," lying there, is set within the context of the universe surrounding them, its larger rhythms at one with the lovers: "under us all moved, and moved us, gently, up and down, and from side to side."

BACK TO THE BOAT (22–23)

Having found the desired passage, Krapp now winds back to its beginning. The usual practice when staging this play is to have all the passages Krapp hears in sequence on the tape. However, I have on one occasion been a bit more daring, forcing the actor to find the passage about the women on his own: that is, recording it only once. This is risky because what will usually happen, given the pressures of performance, is that the actor may overshoot or undershoot the start of the passage. On the other hand, there can be an advantage: the actor's anxiety to stop at the right place duplicates Krapp's own. Thus, the reality of performance is at one with Krapp's eagerness to find that single passage on the tape that, as he says earlier, is one of "those things worth having when all . . . [his] dust has settled."

Having found the beginning of the passage, Krapp relaxes. I held the tape recorder as if I had my arms around a woman, my face serene. If Beckett is the playwright of dark Irish humor, then here he is no less romantic. Delivering this passage, playing this decrepit old man clinging to perhaps the one truly intimate moment in his life, I always thought of that other improbable couple, fat Maddy Rooney and her blind husband in Beckett's *All That Fall*, walking home through the rain, with Maddy's suddenly turning to the irritable old man on, "Put your arm around me. (*Pause.*) Be nice to me" (Beckett 1959, 87). I note also that Mrs. Rooney has been reading Krapp's unsuccessful novel to her husband, for Mr. Rooney speculates that in the next chapter "Effie is going to commit adultery with the Major" (70). Krapp will soon confess to "Scald[ing] his eyes. . . . reading *Effie* again, a page a day, with tears again" (25).

The episode in the boat is a poignant one: both agree that the love affair is now "hopeless." As Krapp, I switched off the tape-recorder, this time quietly, reluctantly, almost reverently. I have replayed this episode every night for the past thirty years, in fact, have made fresh copies of it on other reels to preserve the quality. Hence, "farewell to love" has numerous entries in the ledger.

The woman is long gone, but in my memory she remains as something of a muse, an inspiration. Krapp is at a crossroads. After thirty years of inactivity, witnessing the lethargy of his artistic talent, can he try one more time tonight, inspired by this muse, to create, to make a fresh recording?

A Second, More Desperate Intermission (23–24)

Before exiting, Krapp like a juggler draws three telling objects from the capacious pockets in his overcoat. One is the banana, medicine for his "fatal condition" and a phallic parody of his diminished physical powers. The other two are the watch, reminder both of his advanced years and the significance of tonight, and the envelope, making its third appearance, the rough draft or suggested topics for the new recording. Offstage he downs a drink, then pours but, thinking better of it, does not drink a second one. I came back onstage slightly drunk ("a little unsteadily into light") but not so far gone as to inhibit my imagination. Krapp takes out the virgin reel, loads it, consults the envelope in his pocket, then lays it on the table, "clears his throat and begins to record." I lingered over these moves, avoiding the final one of speaking into the recorder, indeed, was so nervous that, as Beckett's subsequent stage direction indicates, I forgot at first to turn on the recorder.

KRAPP'S CREATION (24–27)

First Krapp corrects his mistake in not turning on the recorder, a comic false start that brought a healthy dose of self-laughter from my Krapp, though Beckett calls only for "brooding". Then, with the recorder properly turned on, he begins the laborious act of creating, throwing out a series of fragments, some poetic, some less so, some sustained, some short-lived. He broods, consults the envelope, then crumples it before tossing it away. He even resorts to adding in the rest of the lyrics from "Now the day is over." The act is clearly a strain: Krapp both "coughs" to the extent of almost losing his voice and "gasps". I thought of Krapp here as a woman in labor, wanting to, trying to expel her child, the pauses serving as the spaces for taking in breath before violently expelling it so as to push the child down the birth canal. When I later directed the play, my actor took a darker reading: for him, Krapp's fragments were like the proverbial "review" of one's life experienced by a drowning man.

The range and variety of topics is extraordinary: the world, a "muck-ball"; Krapp as a little boy, his mind not on his "homework"; the comic linking of "spool" and "stool"; the failed novel, of which only seventeen copies were sold; the old man shivering on a park bench; a lost love, the girl (perhaps the one on the boat) with whom he "could have been happy"; the prostitute Fanny; going to Vespers as a little boy "in short trousers"; and a link with the present, as he urges himself to finish his booze and get to bed.

The collection ends with a dazzling contrast. Krapp sees himself as an old man "wander"ing or "propped up in the dark," his foray into the past only reminding him of "all that old misery." Yet against this stands a joyous memory of a Christmas Eve, gathering "red-berried" holly with his family, hearing sleigh bells in Croghan on a Sunday morning. The word Krapp repeats here is "be," a recognition of, a cry for life, existence, breath—being. Then Krapp adds a coda where he at once chastises himself for wanting to return to his youth, to live his life over ("Once wasn't enough for you"), and invokes, this time in the present, the sensual moment on the boat: "Lie down across her."

The Woman on the Boat Once More (25–26)

As a "reward" for having made the creative effort, my Krapp "indulges" himself by returning once again to the passage about the woman on the boat. I smiled here, a smile of exhaustion and yet tremendous personal satisfaction. Nor did I feel so guilty now about replaying the passage, for the woman, the sensual and creative center of my world, has been "reborn" in the passage just recorded. Fading, perhaps even nonexistent physical powers have been counterbalanced by my art, however halting or fragmented.

My friend Enoch Brater, a marvelous Beckett scholar, told me of visiting the playwright just a few weeks before he died. Having moved out of his apartment, Beckett now lived in a little room close to the hospital where he was being cared for. The new surroundings were sparse: there was a simple cot, a black and white television on the floor to the left, and a small bedstand to the right. On that bedstand, my friend told me, were two books: a copy of Shakespeare's plays and Dante's *Divine Comedy*. *Krapp's Last Tape* is no allegory, nor do I in any way suggest that Dante is its source. But there is a three-part structure to the play: a journey through hell, the darkness and isolation Krapp first feels; the purgatory of confronting his younger self this evening; and at last a fleeting paradise, a return to this Beatrice (a most secular one, to be sure!) who years ago brought him some limited joy. Krapp makes this three-part journey through a prop, the tape recorder or machine of memory.

Live Theater, Past and Present (28)

In an extraordinary merger of man and machine, the physical actor before us with the voice of the actor on that "inner-stage" of the tape recorder on the desk, Krapp moves his lips (or "lip-synchs") to the words recorded thirty years ago and coming from the tape. Refusing to admit the pleasure he took in recalling the episode with the woman, the voice tries to hide under "busy work," announcing he is ending the reel, giving the box and then the spool a number. Admitting "there was a chance of happiness" with the woman, he quickly add a qualification, "But I wouldn't want them back. Not with the fire in me now. No, I wouldn't want them back." As the voice on the tape, I delivered these lines defensively, the subtext being: "I *do* want those moments of happiness. I want them back. But I fear my desires. Such happiness only comes once; it's too much to want it back again. If I cease wanting, I can avoid disappointment, sorrow. Besides, I've wasted myself away in drink ('the fire in me now'). Better just to stay drunk than wish for something in the past, something that only happened once. No, I wouldn't want them back."

Still, as the live actor onstage, mouthing those words, I let come to the surface what was a suppressed subtext for the voice, for my other and earlier half. I thereby showed that I was well aware of this self-deception from the past, of trying to deny what I most desired. Hence, by face, gesture, movement, the actor onstage says: "I do want those moments back. Even if the wish is futile, I want to be again with her on the boat. Listen to that stupid bastard I used to be, probably still am, though perhaps not quite as absurd. Listen to him trying to deny what he wants. Excusing away any chance of happiness." This more affirmative Krapp emerges from the present evening, the presence of the theatre itself; it is the Krapp who has taken that unused reel from the drawer, rather than shutting it away as in the past, and has made a recording, re-igniting his dormant imagination. Once referring to the warmth of the drink, the "fire in" him now takes on a second meaning: the impulse for creation. The live actor before us has come to terms with, in a sense used the recorded voice on the play's most graphic prop, the tape recorder.

5

Building a Character's History

SUBTEXT INCLUDES NOT ONLY THE INTERNAL VOICE OF A CHARACTER, that hidden self influencing the actual stage dialogue, but the character's history, his or her life before and outside the play proper. Now, some actors are content just to "play the dialogue," to work with what is there on the page. Others imagine that the character we see onstage is only the tip of the iceberg, perhaps the most fascinating tip, but still not the full character. In creating a history for the character the actor thereby fleshes out a personality created by the playwright. We do what the six visitors ask of the director and his cast in Pirandello's *Six Characters in Search of an Author*. Usually during the third week of rehearsals, my actors and I will sit down and share the histories of the characters, what their lives were like from birth until the present. Once shared, these histories elicit questions from fellow actors: what would your character do in such and such a situation? what does she think of this pressing issue? what is his favorite color? Questions large and small. One director friend has actors do improvisations based on their characters, putting them in situations sometimes related to, sometimes unlike situations in the play itself. I knew an actor who spent two weeks in a law firm as preparation for playing a lawyer onstage. An actor who had the role of Bert in Pinter's *The Room* traveled around for a week in the van of a delivery driver. The paradox is that such histories, albeit fictive, lend a sense of reality to the onstage enactment. I created such as history for myself when I played Saul Kimmer in a production of Shepard's *True West*.[1]

THE SCHOLARS' TAKE ON SAUL

Cast in the relatively small role of the slick Hollywood producer, I was determined to make my Saul Kimmer as interesting as possible. I had only two scenes in the play, but I remembered the theatrical cliché: there are no small parts, only small actors.

The "old man" of the cast, my first impulse was to play Saul as a would-be father, first to Austin, then Lee. Saul, as I saw the character, needed one of the boys, for while successful in the past, he had been hit by a series of failures for five years now: options not picked up, projects dropped for lack of sponsors, films that flopped at the box office. He sees Austin, then Lee as his ticket back to the big time. This is what Saul admits to himself; that he also wants a son is a subtexual desire.

I also took advice from an actor friend who told me, "I cherish my character's ego: for him, whatever happens onstage is the way he sees it. No one else, not even the leads, has his vision." What I told my friend was "productive arrogance" on his part would, I felt, help me with Saul, for if he is down on his luck, he is a fighter, waiting for a comeback, and willing to do anything that needs to be done for that moment, even gambling away Austin's contract on the golf links with Lee. Also, my Saul had that sense of superiority that older men sometimes display around younger men, even if its source is a defensive envy of their youth.

Playing a minor role, not having the myriad responsibilities of being a director, would also give me time to think about the rest of the play. I had the leisure of contemplating not only the director's concept but the wealth of scholarly commentary on Shepard and *True West*. Following Brecht's principles, I wanted to see where Saul fit within the larger play, what, beyond his own comprehension, he "meant" in that pattern sustained by scenes in which he does not appear.

With few exceptions, the commentary on *True West* essentially allegorizes the work: Lee and Austin, and to a lesser extent Saul Kimmer and the Mother, represent something beyond themselves. Such allegory is especially appropriate for Shepard, indeed is invited by the playwright, despite his claim in the long note to scene 1 that the "evolution of the characters' situation . . . is the most important focus of the play" (Shepard 3).

Certainly, such evolution is the focus for *True West*'s four actors charged with making the characters credible moment by moment. That reversal in roles between the leads in act 2, for example, must follow convincingly from what the playwright, director, and the actors have established in act 1. This same evolution holds for the audience as well for, by definition, they cannot think retroactively while a performance is in progress. For both actor and audience, then, the characters, however complex, simply "are." Part of their charm is that Lee and Austin do not think of themselves as part of a larger plan.

Like the scholars, however, Shepard has other plans for the brothers. I think of him as the Herman Melville of the American theater, trying to write "the great American play," one that will embody his own concerns about the dysfunctional family, the clash in values between the imagined West and the contemporary suburbs, the ways the artist navigates between truth and the illusion of truth. *A Lie of the Mind*, *Curse of the Starving Class*, *Buried Child*, and most certainly *True West*—the titles themselves announce this larger, extradramatic function. For all his realism, the everyday dialogue, the sets filled with the detritus of American consumer society, the present world of small-time crooks, hustlers, neurotic mothers, indifferent fathers, quarreling siblings, recognizable places, and name brands, Shepard more than inclines toward allegory. Consider the American flag wrapped around the rifle in *A Lie of the Mind*, the eagle and the cat locked in combat in *Curse of the Starving Class*, or Tilden at the end of *Buried Child* carrying onstage the dead baby. To this allegory scholars and critics have been especially sensitive.

Austin and Lee, in their readings, constitute the poles of the play, elemental forces locked in "mutual repulsion" (Bottoms 1998, 193), two fighters whom the director Robert Woodruff describes as performing a "complicated, savage, violent dance" (Oumano 1986, 137). They are antitheses: mind and body, creature of words and creature of action, "reality and art" (Hall 1993, 105), symbol of the romanticized West and the demoralized American suburbs, the domesticated "cricket" and the savage "coyote" (Tucker 1992, 136), a once-single man now divided against himself and thereby displaying the "erosion of belief structures and the duress suffered by the American family" (Wade 1992, 103). Incomplete, separated from their other half, each longs to be the other: Austin, coveting Lee's power, instinct, savagery, freedom; Lee, Austin's sophistication, family life, intellect, restraint. They gravitate between two settings: the father's "mystical western world of manliness, rootlessness, and violence" and "the world of mom and her kitchen" (Auberbach 1988, 57). Embodying the good and bad in man, they combine the instincts toward creation and destruction, "tussling in metaphysical territory" (Shewly 1985, 140), players in an updated western, alternately wearing those generic white and black hats, and dueling at "the final showdown" in scene 9 (McDonough 1997, 50). That ambiguous ending, where Lee, supposedly dead, suddenly comes to life as the brothers "square off to each other . . . caught in a vast desert-like landscape" (59), has the "Brechtian air of epic alienation," and we as audience cannot resolve the paradox of this "after image" (Tucker 1992, 140).

Standing backstage, I had the advantage of simultaneously hearing and thinking about my fellow actors, Lee and Austin, as each night they engaged in this allegorical struggle, switching places in the second act and thereby enacting the "two selves of the artist" (Tucker 1992, 137), man of action and man of language. But all these allegorical readings had to be abandoned once I stepped onstage as Saul, especially Saul for, even more than the brothers, he is not self-critical, let alone meta-critical. With no idea of what he represents, Saul is only interested in the deal or, in his words as he speaks in the corporate executive's impersonal third person plural, a "project that we feel has commercial potential" (18). Tell Saul he has a need for a son, and he'd think you were crazy, or some egghead intellectual.

I found Saul sensitive to anything regarding himself, but insensitive to whatever was outside his own needs. Bonnie Marranca suggests he may be able to respond to something deeper in Lee's story when he speaks of it as having the "ring of truth" (Marranca 1981, 123; Shepard 1981, 35). Perhaps. Or he may just mean "truth" in the producer's sense of the movie's having an effect on the audience.

Austin tells Lee that Saul "thinks [the brothers are] the same person" (37), but I don't think the reported line necessarily signals Saul's "making explicit" the notion that they are the "two selves of the artist" which ultimately "do not cohere" (Tucker 1992, 137). Saul is no Brechtian onlooker. Austin's object in this line is to wound Lee, now that Saul has transferred allegiances between the brothers. Deep down, he may even be using Saul's calling them "one and the same" to draw closer to Lee, an early signal for Austin's desperate plan to live with Lee in the desert. In any case, Lee sees through Austin, dismissing him with a curt "Don't get cute." Austin may even be inventing the line. Surely characters can sometimes say more than they intend; they can also embody a larger social, allegorical, or psychological type of which they are unaware. Whether intended or not, Austin's line can be important in that retrospective act of interpretation, invited, as I have argued, by this playwright whose works graphically play out the contradictions of American culture. But I do not think Saul has such consciousness.

Again, this is not to say that Saul does not represent a type within that allegorical polarity established by the brothers. In fact, in my attempt to stand outside my character, both during rehearsals and once the character was set in performance, I profited from the commentary on Saul.

Some critics dismiss Saul as a caricature, more type than person. One of the world's "big executives" (McDonough 1997, 49), the "virtual embodiment of [the medium's] system of re-production and consumption" (Rabillard 1993, 87), he epitomizes "the hollow artifice" (Bottoms 1998, 201) of Hollywood society. Yet if he is "bluntly two-dimensional as a character, . . . he nevertheless [is] a type recognizable to anyone who has sat at a business meeting or ordered fast food" (Bottoms 1998, 201). Saul champions the "Hollywood dream-trade" (Orr 1991, 148) to which Austin and Lee both aspire, and hence he has the power to "reverse the brothers' societal positions" (Wade 1992, 104). If Austin in his sensitivity to language and Lee in his Hemingway-like experience with raw life encompass the two prerequisites for genuine artistic creation, Saul corrupts both with his demand that "scripts [be written] according to . . . cut and dried formulas" (Orbinson 1987, 193). Driven solely by the marketplace, Saul's perversion of "subject matter . . . holds the author prisoner" (Rabillard 1993, 90). In an especially perceptive character study, Stephen Bottoms observes that Saul's is not the "monstrous, cartoon power-mania" of other Hollywood types in Shepard, yet he is "disturbing precisely because he is so believable." With his "happy smiling insincerity" and "plastic bonhomie," Saul offers only a "smile [that] is the mask which has become real" (Bottoms 1998, 210). He is the "tight-lipped, business-like" man who "gambles with Austin's livelihood and loses" (DeRose 1992, 111). Parodying Lee, the "natural man" or the villain of the West, Saul is the bandit of Hollywood and Vine, driven, despite his surface charm, by "less civilized emotions," so much so that Lee taps into his "fear and greed" (DeRose 110). John Orr calls Lee's victory over Saul on the golf course an instance of "bi-sexual hustling" (Orr 1991, 149). If the "passing on of power" from their absent father to Lee and Austin proves "only an illusion," or a "patrimony [that] exists in the mind" (Tucker 139), then Saul stands as the new father, bestowing and then taking away power that is even more illusory given its Hollywood source. Dealing with two surrogate sons, Saul thus mocks that father-figure who is the "apex of the triad of the West" (Tucker 1992, 140). In this light, Saul, as father figure, is balanced at the end of the play by the Mother who, no less illusory, is "just as Lee and Austin have 'scripted' her—a mother, not an individual" (Hall 1993, 105). Little wonder both brothers, this Cain and Abel (Tucker 1992, 138), are drawn toward Saul, for his belief system, if it can be called that, is that "people go to the movies for the illusion of truth" (Mottram 1997, 47).

A Personal History for Saul

I patterned Saul after those colorful hucksters I knew as a young boy in my blue-collar neighborhood in South Philadelphia. Men like my father, a telephone installer, were the respectable norm; they had wives and children and lived in row houses with front porches where on Friday and Saturday nights parents would sit drinking Schmidt's beer, gossiping up and down the rows, while we kids played stickball in the streets. The hucksters were a different breed. Most often without wives, and hence children, they lived in the rooming houses that dotted the neighborhood. With rare exception, they did not have a job in the sense that my father did. No, they were always in pursuit of some sweet deal, some "kill" just around the corner, a project that would reverse not only their present low fortunes but those of anyone willing to put up some cash and join them. The hucksters were ubiquitous. They'd approach my father and his buddies in the appropriately named Hollywood Tavern (our local bar), at political meetings, at my Uncle Mickey's barber shop, on the street.

They had a thinly disguised contempt for "squares" with real jobs. With their fancy clothes, suits that had a sheen, fedoras, loud ties, and heavy gold cufflinks, they distinguished themselves from telephone workers and the lot in their drab pants and white Sears shirts. But the fact is that none of these hucksters ever really made that big killing; they just talked about it. They were always on the verge of success. In fact, it was the expectation of success that was their stimulant. They were like that vaudevillian spinning ten dinner plates on long sticks, the lure of the act being the performer's frantic rushing from plate to plate, correcting a wobble here, restarting a plate about to fall there. Having all ten plates rotate simultaneously was only a by-product.

When you looked closely at the huckster's outfit you could see that his tie was stained, the collar frayed, the pants didn't quite match the jacket. It was all a dream of consummating the "big one." The huckster survived by fabricating that success which was eternally tomorrow; he was a living chain letter, an illusionist making his living by drawing the unsuspecting worker into his world of play. My dad was so drawn on three occasions, and I recall my mother screaming melodramatically at him one night, "Why won't you ever learn? Why?" I had a mixed contempt and awe for the huckster. He was my earliest introduction to the theater, to the craft of the actor.

Saul, for me, is one of these hucksters, and doubly so for the product he sells is not that shipment unloaded yesterday on the docks or the sure-fire option on that vacant lot just off Broad Street's business district. No, his product is the movies from the justly named Hollywood dream factory. I simply transferred the huckster to the streets of downtown LA.

Saul's past box-office successes had very much to do with his own relentless publicity of his projects, creating the illusion that the film was a "must see." But now, for the past five years, Saul has had a string of failures. Immune to any self-criticism, not a man given to introspection, he cannot, does not, want to explore the reasons for this sudden fall. Instead, he blames it on suprahuman forces, on "them," a fickle public, anything but himself. Predictably, he has been drinking heavily; for two days before his appointment with Austin he has been dead drunk. Saul just manages to sober up in time for the meeting. He comes to Austin, rather than Austin's coming to him, but Saul justifies this by labeling it a "charity visit" to a struggling scriptwriter, an instance where the great man condescends to enter the house of the less fortunate. What can kill Saul, what can kill the huckster, is to lose that faith in illusion, in the ability to refashion one's self fresh each day. As long as the possibility for success exists, Saul exists.

Looking at these hucksters floating on their dreams like the table levitated by the mystic, I felt there was something perversely noble about them. Creators of a fraudulent world, they are creators nevertheless. Saul is loved by no one, and in a rare moment of introspection he may realize this. But he cannot think of himself as a failure. To strip away the layers of self-deceit, rationalization, illusion, artifice, shallowness, would kill him. And there's little chance of that.

SAUL IN SCENE 3 (15–19)

Shepard has Saul dressed in a "pink and white flower print sports shirt, white sports coat with matching polyester slacks, black and white loafers" (2). We took some liberties with this. My Saul wore a conservative blue jacket, recently laundered but still showing its wear around the collar and cuffs. The dark blue pants almost matched; he had a conservative shirt but a gaudy tie that just didn't fit. Perhaps Hollywood producers do not usually visit writers in their homes, but my Saul is down on his luck, desperate to score. Violating custom, therefore, he arrives at Austin's house dressed as nicely as he can, purposely distinguishing himself from the producer stereotype in sports shirt: he wants to create the image of a wise, conservative older man, not that of a salesman. Though he's been drinking heavily, in the opening conversation before Lee enters he tries to hide the fact, believing he can conceal a hangover better than he actually does. Saul cradles his drink, nursing it, knowing it would violate that conservative image to ask for a second one.

I sat close to Austin, enjoying the intimacy, lavishing praise on him: the young writer has "really managed to capture something this time." At the same time Saul strokes his own ego: Austin needs him, for it will take someone with Saul's connections to "make a sale to television," getting a "major star . . . someone bankable." Austin has some talent; I envy him that, and this fact only drives me to impress on him how much he needs me. I like playing the Polonius, giving out advice: Austin is not to "touch the typewriter until we have some seed money." I will protect him from the cutthroat world of Hollywood. I am also not above using him, "riding him" as far as his talent will take me.

Lee's entrance ("abruptly" in the stage direction) shatters this idyll. Knowing he has to size up this intruder quickly since Lee somehow threatens him, Saul draws on what we called in South Philadelphia "street smarts," putting on his plastic smile, offering Lee the platitudes of the perfect guest, all the while guarding himself. He rises and stands awkwardly between the two brothers, and when Lee tosses back his platitudes, Saul knows this intruder is his opponent. Lee, of course, has been spoiling for a fight with Saul since the last scene, for Austin's wanting to be alone with the producer only hypes the competition between the brothers: "[You want me to] pound the pavement for a few hours while you bullshit yer way into a million bucks" (13). In our production Lee made it quite clear that his entry was not accidental; he hears that initial conversation between Austin and Saul from the porch, then enters on cue. To Austin, his "Aw shit, I'm sorry about that" smacks of insincerity, an insincerity which Saul also detects.

And so now Saul and Lee, under the guise of the polite conversation between people newly introduced, pull out the knives. Lee's mispronouncing Saul's last name as "Kipper" may be an accident, but as Saul I took it as intentional, and my abrupt corrective "Kimmer" was almost scolding, so much so that Austin must intervene to move the conversation to a new topic. Saul and Lee are boxers, early in the match, testing out each other. I mention the "Bob Hope Drive," assuming Lee has no commerce with such fancy places. He does, or claims he does. I assume he doesn't play golf, the rich man's sport; again, he parries me by claiming he does. Lee pushes me into a golf match, nor is he deterred when Austin once again tries to change the topic to Alaska. I don't believe Lee plays golf, but I can't take the chance, and so toss out the self-deprecating "I'm just a Sunday duffer really," which he matches with "That's good 'cause I haven't swung a club in months." I lose this first round, however, when he pushes me to set a date for the game. And he sees through my shallow "Sounds really great."

I fear Lee and yet am somehow attracted to him. He's a fellow street fighter, a huckster. Indeed, as it turns out, the golf match will be a true con job, the event divorcing Saul from Austin. Nevertheless, there is an energy about Lee, a sexuality and power that Saul admires, understands. In contrast, Austin now seems dull, without spirit. Lee crosses to me, putting Austin on stage left, as he suggests a subordinate role for his brother as "our caddie." Increasingly attracted to Lee, I am no less in contention with him: when he suggests that his brother could "pick . . . up" the techniques of golf in "fifteen minutes," I support him with "Sure. Doesn't take long." But then I pointedly add that "you have to play for years to find your true form." I took the "chuckles" in Shepard's stage direction to myself, the subtext being: "this fellow thinks he's a hotshot, and maybe he is. But I've got years on him—years." Saul is beginning to experience what I called in my actor's notebook "a loving condescension" for Lee. On his part, Lee cements our relationship by belittling his brother. Sometimes direct, more often implied, a collective "we" creeps into his dialogue: "We'll give ya' a quick run-down on the club faces"; "[We'll] show ya' a couple points"; "[We] might even let ya' hit."

When Lee puts his arm around me, I feel a little claustrophobic, even as I like this physical contact. We flirted in rehearsals with the idea of Saul's having a homosexual feeling for Lee, a feeling that Lee senses and then plays on when he pictures the men, after a round of gold, taking a "hot shower" and "snappin' towels at each other's privates. Real sense a' fraternity." While we never pursued this option, I think it remained there, subtextually, but less powerful than the growing father/son connection between Saul and Lee which has supplanted that between Saul and Austin. Saul still needs to flaunt his social superiority: he will "call the country club" to set a golf date. Yet clearly he is drawn to Lee.

Lee reads Saul perfectly, and tries a new strategy as he abandons the "aggressive son" or "fellow huckster" images and poses as the naive student asking Saul about his work. Still recovering from Lee's assault, I don't detect a setup as I launch into a boast about my present work, shading the truth that my career has been dormant for some time: I "fooled" around with television "in the past," producing some television specials, with the reminder that it was "network stuff," as opposed to local television. But "it's mainly features now." This claim to be working on pictures is undercut, however, by the "mainly": the last feature was five years ago; the "mainly" is much more past than present.

I need time to assess Lee, what he's after. As he is about to cross to the upstage-right door, Lee catches Saul with, "Austin was tellin' me that yer interested in stories." Saul is on his guard, not because he's uninterested in good scripts but rather because he's not sure he has the power anymore to deliver on projects, whether good or bad. He depends not just on merit but also luck, connections, the present reputation of the producer, a host of factors that he cannot control. Thus, Saul retreats behind "business-speak": "Well, we develop certain projects that we feel have commercial potential." Saul believes, or wants to believe that Lee needs him, and so brushes him off with "Sometimes" when he asks Saul if he "go[es] in for . . . westerns." Saul heads for the door again, eagerly, on Austin's "I'll give you a ring, Saul."

As he tries to exit, however, Lee closes in, literally blocking him from leaving. In our production he put his arm around me, taking me to stage-right, as far from Austin as possible. In the ensuing conversation about westerns he slowly led me from upstage to downstage right, his arm tight around my shoulder, his face a mere inch away. The entry in my actor's notebook called this "Lee's stroll": I felt like a woman being led by an aggressive man, feeling at once secure with him but also a little scared. Our Lee almost pressed his face against mine, the way young children often talk to adults, not knowing those social conventions dictating a proper space between the parties. I have a strong voice, and most certainly had used it earlier in the scene as I played both the condescending father with Austin and the dual polite guest/fellow street fighter with Lee. Now that voice fell almost to a whisper, as if I were a straight man to Lee and nothing more. "He is stealing my voice," I put in my notes. As Lee unveils to Saul his idea about a "Western that'd knock yer lights out," a "contemporary" story that is "True life," Saul is reduced to "Oh reallys" and "wells" and "I suppose sos". Austin is almost out of the picture, confined to a single "Yes" from stage left when Lee asks if he's seen the movie *Lonely Are the Brave*.

Outlining the plot, then focusing on the moment when Kirk Douglas dies inwardly as he realizes his horse is dead, Lee's longish speech conquers Saul. Despite its mawkish plot, Lee's intensity here, his sense of conviction, again steals my voice. I literally found myself holding my breath for the nine lines of the speech, becoming an audience giving what my notes called a "reverent silence" for the performer. Only when Lee releases Saul and he begins to make his way to the exit upstage right can he return to solid ground, those clichés that have been his stock and trade, his way of "greasing" through life, as a colleague calls it: "Well, it sounds like a great movie" and "I'll have to try to catch it some time." Lee now stands smirking as Saul tries to regain his dignity: adjusting his collar, making a few stabs at conversation, acting as if nothing had happened. Saul's "arrange a screening or something" has as a subtext: "I'm still superior to this young fellow." His justification for having to leave because of the freeway rush-hour traffic, though, has the sound of desperation.

With a little space between Saul and Lee who, crossing halfway to shake my hand, was at stage center, Saul can return to that social self at which he is adept, the shallow persona that helps him ward off everything from victorious competitors in the business to thoughts about his own string of failures. Lee even returns to the pose of the naive student with "So ya' think there's room for a real Western these days?" and the falsely modest, "You'd take a look at it then?" Saul senses the setup, the fake courtesy and posturing of a fellow huckster, and is eager to reassert the image of the successful, experienced Hollywood producer: "I don't see why not" or "I'll give it a read-through," or the cloying modesty of "It would just be my opinion, of course." His "Why don't you—uh—tell the story to Austin and have him write a little outline?" only reveals Saul's weakness. His reclaiming the hardheaded producer is just a "gift" from Lee as he suffers Saul to return to his accustomed role.

Saul glances back at the brothers as if to say, "Have I just been had?" Late in rehearsals I added a sigh combining relief with exhaustion. The audience laughed at this, as if they understood, as if they felt the comedy of this man who enters posing as a conqueror and exits the victim or loser. Austin and Lee took a long beat after Saul left, and when Austin turns to Lee with "Give me the keys," his attempt to assert his authority backfires. Lee, in Shepard's stage direction, "doesn't move, just stares at Austin, smiles." Our lighting operator took a fast fade to black.

SAUL IN SCENE 6 (32–36)

When Saul returns in scene 6 of act 2, much has changed. The two intervening scenes, one before, the other after intermission, move the brothers from bonding together as they collaborate on the script to quarreling violently when Austin learns that Saul has dropped his script and picked up the outline for Lee's western. Positions now reversed, Austin is the outcast. But if Lee "wins" the first act, and wins again in scene 6 with Saul, he will fall apart once Saul leaves and he is forced to assume the task of the writer. The play starts leveling off after Saul's exit. Feeling that Shepard let Lee outplay him in act 1, our Austin could now assert himself: stealing toasters, getting drunk, taking pleasure in Lee's discomfort, becoming as witty and vocal in scenes 7 and 8 as Lee commanded the stage in the previous act. Saul can transfer power to Lee, but such power is illusory. In a very basic sense, the real battle is domestic. Can the brothers forge a love in the midst of their differences, aggravated as they are by a dysfunctional family (the absent father, the mother gone to Alaska) and a society that in the person of Saul values raw power, material success, and illusion over truth?

At the top of the scene Saul was stage left, Lee sitting on the kitchen counter upstage center, and Austin stage right slumped at the table. This time, when Lee mispronounces Saul's name, the correction is genial. Feeling a little guilty at dropping Austin and picking up Lee's option, Saul is wise enough to know that Lee needs Austin to get the script into shape. I delivered Saul's announcement that he wants to continue with Austin's project "too" as an outright lie: he will quickly admit that "we can't do both." Saul overplays his hand now when he suggests that the brothers' "familiarity with the material" makes Austin indispensable. Austin rejects that argument, then brands Saul a fellow "hustler" along with Lee, while granting his brother the status of the "bigger hustler." When Austin bolts from the table stage left with, "I'm the one who wrote the fuckin' outline," I instinctively move closer to Lee: it is now two against one.

Saul fears that his big chance is being jeopardized: he has Lee, but he also needs Austin. He tries to remain calm but there is an edge in his voice. Having failed on the argument about the brothers' familiarity, he now tries with desperate complements to convince Austin to stay with the project: "We have big studio money standing behind this thing. Just on the basis of your outline." He even hits on the strategy of using some of the money to support the father: he and Lee have planned a trust fund for the old man which Lee has "volunteered" to administer. Austin, however, rejects all of Saul's lures. Saul in turn feels the fish about to slip off the hook. In truth, whatever attraction Lee may have, the only thing driving Saul now is self-preservation. Austin pushes us into a corner with, "There's no way I'm doing it"; Shepard indicates a "long pause" before Saul speaks.

The Saul emerging from that pause is not "new"; we have heard and seen vestiges of this side of him earlier, but never so graphically. Moving toward center stage, using my hands to craft each word as if I were carving them out of the air, I wanted to impress Austin with just how big a deal awaits us, all three, or even just the two of us. Wounding him for disobedience with "Now you've never been offered that kind of money before," I gave Lee's knee a fatherly pat, designed to hurt Austin, on "Your brother has really got something, Austin. I've been around too long not to recognize it. Raw talent." But what really drives Saul here is the optimistic picture of a possible score. As he speaks of how "incredible" it is that three studios are "all trying to cut each other's throats to get this material," adding "in one morning," that they are bidding just on the basis of a "first draft," he pictures himself back in the loop, being fawned on by starlets, courted by fellow producers. For a moment Lee and Austin cease to exist for him; Austin's "I'm not writing it" brings Saul back to reality.

Saul operates very differently in this second scene of act 2. In the first act he begins confidently, then, caught between attraction and repulsion, is unsettled by Lee as he alternates between competing with the younger man and taking refuge in Hollywood clichés. In act 1 Saul draws on various parts of himself, either as needed for his image or as weapons against the competition. Induced by Lee with his trick of playing the naive student, Saul counters with the condescending producer. Thus, after that initial conversation alone with Austin, Saul is not one but several complementary beings. In act 1, scene 3 Shepard seems to be parceling out aspects of Saul's character on which the actor might play variations.

Saul appears more "layered" here in act 2, and as each layer is expended, both the actor and the audience get closer to his center. Until the pause before his "I See. Well—" Saul has been, in this order: ingratiating yet also stern with Austin, frenzied as he sees the project failing without Austin, devious in the scheme to set up a trust fund for the father, and self-centered as he recalls the studios' fighting over the script. What we now get is "the real Saul," stripped of the social niceties that lubricate his dealings with the world, a naked ego beyond compassion, let alone any fraternal feelings.

In a calm, determined voice, cruel in that it lacks passion, Saul dismisses Austin the way one would flick lint off a coat. His "I'm sorry about this, Austin" is painfully insincere, as is his "I wish there was another way." Austin is the son who has betrayed the father, and so when Austin asks, "What do you see in it?" I crossed back to Lee, putting that fatherly hand on his shoulder, drawing him closer. Whether Saul means what he says, that Lee's story has "the ring of truth," that it captures "the real West," that he is "speaking from experience," is almost beside the point. While it may expose his distorted Hollywood sense of reality, and of the West, the object of the lines is to hurt Austin. He is a parent playing off one child against the other. A dismissive wave of the hand is accompanied by "But nobody's interested in love these days, Austin. Let's face it." There are no friendships in Saul's world.

If Saul is ever capable of seeing himself, it is here when the layers are stripped away and that coldness at his core exposed. By his own admission, he operates on his "instincts," his "gut reaction," taking "gambles" in life on his "hunches." And if Saul lies to Austin and himself when he claims he's "never been wrong," at this moment he so perfectly exposes his true self, the naked, unaccommodated man, that he admits no lie in the boast.

Several members of the audience said they felt a "chill" in Saul's simple exit line, "I have to go now, Austin." Austin too feels this coldness in Saul, as he shouts out that the producer is "dried up," a "dead issue," just like the belief that there is "such [a] thing as the West anymore." As Saul, I thought of letting Austin's remark go, but then paused, my hand on the door knob, before turning around. The competitor in Saul can't resist hitting back. However, instead of at first trying to wound Austin, I tipped my hat to him with the caveat "But I have to take the gamble, don't I?" Saul endures, schemes, plans, convinces himself and us that one of those sweet deals is just around the corner, just like those pathetic yet somehow *heroic* hucksters I knew as a boy.

If Saul ever holds the stage, taking the attention away from the two brilliant lead characters, it comes when he says, "I've always gone on my hunches. Always. And I've never been wrong." For just a second, the audience could see the cold middle-aged man underneath the oil and gloss of this dream salesman. I felt that, until I left the stage, Austin had been killed by Saul, or drained of life.

Saul's final lines to Lee, however, start to unravel his "victory." This was my take on the character. He still needs Lee's affection, his approval. Every victory for Saul is short-lived, each success becoming its own devil's advocate, every big project progressively losing its luster with each second after consummation. Saul's object in telling Lee "I'll talk to you tomorrow" may be to hurt Austin, but it seems less an order, less the "Don't call us; we'll call you" formula of the Hollywood bigwig than a plea, a cry for reassurance. On his part, Lee responds like an equal with "All right, Mr. Kimmer," rather than a young man needing to please. Wanting a more grateful reaction, Saul tries to press the connection with "Maybe we could have some lunch," yet Lee's "Fine with me" was more mechanical than enthusiastic. Saul's final "I'll give you a ring" is a bit neurotic, almost redundant since he has already said he would "talk to [Lee] tomorrow." If I left the stage in scene 3 confused, trying to assess what Lee has done to me, here I exited with an anxious question: would Lee stay with me? Having dismissed Austin, can I still count on the other brother?

Saul's change of allegiance affects the brothers for the next three scenes. His addiction to Hollywood, to finding success in creating illusions, to thinking of "art" only as a commercial project corrupts both Austin and Lee. Conversely, set adrift from their family, trying to find themselves without a mother and father, or a society of permanent values, they also choose to be corrupted. Saul's history, as I had fashioned it, had informed his presence and his dialogue onstage. Together, past and present remained as a force after Saul had exited, the actor disrobing, standing backstage and listening to the rest of the performance.

6

Playing the Subtext: Pinter's *The Lover*
and *A Kind of Alaska*

IN PINTER, I THINK WHAT COUNTS MOST IS THE PLAY THAT ISN'T QUITE
there, and by this I mean that almost all of the real dialogue is there in
the subtext: the character's history, what he or she is thinking, those
unvarnished lines hidden underneath the text on the page. Pinter's own
metaphor for this subtext is "the weasel under the whiskey cabinet"
(Gussow 1971a, 42–43, 126–36). We approach the cabinet with the
perfunctory task of fetching a bottle of whiskey, but as we unlock the
glass door, we remember that a weasel lives under the cabinet. We
never see the creature; we only know it is there. And so, what would
otherwise be routine, an action without larger meaning, cannot remain
so, for what is hidden beneath the surface, the unknown, invests a very
mundane action with what Pinter in *Old Times* calls "ripples [of mean-
ing] that pervade the surface" (Pinter 1971, 37). Elsewhere, Pinter
speaks of dialogue as "stratagems to cover nakedness."[1] Samuel Beckett, to whom Pinter regularly submitted manuscripts for his judgment,
calls this subtext the "third" or "dark zone," our most profound
thoughts, what we really mean, what we really are, feelings for which
stage dialogue is at best an imperfect translation (Beckett 1957, 111–
12).

Pinter's *The Lover* and *A Kind of Alaska* run the gamut of such subtext,
suggesting this play that isn't quite there. Until its midpoint, *The Lover*
has all the appearance of a British drawing-room comedy where a married couple have an "arrangement" by which the wife's lover visits
while the husband is at work. When the husband Richard reappears as
Max, the lover, we are in on the secret: everything Richard and Sarah
have said to this point, every line of dialogue we have heard, every gesture, every bit of stage business now has a different meaning, one there
all the time but hidden from us or, rather, hidden to the degree that
Richard and Sarah have managed to conceal their true feelings from

each other. No less, it is hidden to the degree that the actors charged with the two parts have to conceal their real object from the audience.

In *A Kind of Alaska* Deborah, a victim of *encephalitis lethargica* or sleeping sickness, emerges from a twenty-nine-year coma, during which time she has been aware of her surroundings but incapable of speech or unaided movement. Without words, buried beneath a subtext, in essence, extending from girlhood to middle age, she now bursts forth with all that hidden dialogue, the account of an invalid's world that has gone unheard until now and whose complexity is almost beyond the comprehension of her listeners, her physician Hornby and Pauline, her sister who has married him.

By good chance I directed productions of both plays within six months of each other.[2] My challenge, the challenge for anyone doing these plays, was how to find and then convey Pinter's subtext. If it is ignored in *The Lover*, the work comes off as a shallow British comedy, the sort of vacuous stuff in which Pinter himself appeared when he was a struggling actor in the provinces. *The Lover* is based on a theatrical game played by husband and wife; if it is to be something more than just another piece about "the business" or a pleasant metadrama, it will be the subtext that elevates the work. There on the surface, and hence subtext that makes its way into the text, it cannot be ignored in *A Kind of Alaska*: the question is, can the actor playing Deborah, and her director, make sense of what she says? There is no doubt about the serious, or even real-life basis of *A Kind of Alaska*: Pinter's source is a case history in Oliver Sacks's *Awakenings*, the physician's account of his bringing back to consciousness with the drug L-DOPA patients suffering from sleeping sickness. The question here is: how can the admittedly fictive dialogue, inspired by a true story, be used to develop the complex characters of Deborah, Hornby, and Pauline, who form the play's unusual *menage à trois*?

"Is Your Lover Coming Today?"

The Lover's opening scene is a perfect example of the multiple blending of subtext, each character's surface object as expressed in the immediate dialogue, and his or her real object as conveyed by the actor through subtextual choices. The concomitant response of the audience is to two plays, one present and another almost there. Because the scene is so short, I quote it in full:

Richard. (Amiably.) Is your lover coming today?
Sarah. Mmnn.
Richard. What time?
Sarah. Three.
Richard. Will you be going out . . . or staying in?
Sarah. Oh . . . I think we'll stay in.
Richard. I thought you wanted to go to that exhibition.
Sarah. I did, yes . . . but think I'd prefer to stay in with him today.
Richard. Mmnn-hmmmm. Well, I must be off. (*Richard goes to hall U.C. and puts on his bowler hat.*) Will he be staying long, do you think?
Sarah. Mmmnnn . . .
Richard. About . . . six, then.
Sarah. Yes.
Richard. Have a pleasant afternoon.
Sarah. Mmnn.
Richard. Bye-bye.

What can be concluded here by the "naive audience," as Marvin Rosenberg has termed it (Rosenberg 1997, 15–55): banal dialogue coupled with a racy situation. Richard seems perfectly happy with the arrangement; the playwright even gives a rare character note: Richard asks the opening question "amiably." Perhaps there is a hint of tension in his having assumed the lovers were going out, rather than staying in, but Sarah, while not disputing the fact, politely reverses herself by saying that she "think[s]" she'd "prefer to stay in today." The perfect, uptight British businessperson, Richard asks if the lover will be staying long. Scratching the surface, we might want to find a subtext here of: "I hope he won't stay the full three hours; I'm happy with, perhaps resigned to her lovemaking, but three hours seems a bit excessive. I hope she'll tell me the lover will only be an hour today—at best two." Sarah's "Mmmnnn" suggests he will stay long, the full three hours. Perhaps somewhat disappointed by her answer, Richard nevertheless recovers quickly. In the hesitation (Pinter's three dots) before his "six" he may think of throwing out five or five-thirty as a reasonable definition of "long," but, sensitive to his wife's feelings, decides after a beat on "six"—the maximum. The scene ends with the clichés of parting.

Now, if this were all we had, if it were, say, one of Pinter's two-page exercises for actors, we could flesh out a history here: the husband is tiring a bit of the arrangement, exposing, but with that wonderful British reserve, a slight irritation. Still not getting the response he wanted, he suppresses his feelings, stiff upper lip and all that.

Of course, as the actors and their director know, as the audience will find out halfway through this short play, the situation is other than meets the eye and ear. As I suggest above, the actors have a choice to make: how much of the full subtext, the true story behind this seeming arrangement, should they reveal to the audience? By definition, such revelation must be subtle, conveyed not in the banal text but through their delivery, more often than not conveyed visually: a gesture, a facial expression, a choice in the blocking. For example, does Richard cross downstage, facing away from Sarah seated upstage right on a divan, for his "I thought you wanted to go to that exhibition?" She would hear only a fairly innocuous question, while the audience could see Richard's slightly pained expression as he hopes she will confirm the original plans of going out. Knowing their heavy lovemaking is confined to in-doors, he hopes that at worst there will be some sensual hand-holding while touring the galleries.

The basis for the "real" subtext growing out of the game they play comes from whatever history the actors devise for the couple. Given the four-week norm for rehearsals, I can usually devote one, at best two days to tablework: sitting around with the actors discussing the play, not yet worrying about lines or blocking. With *The Lover* we spent four days at the table, along with several additional days of individual con-versations, during which time we wrote a history of the marriage, stretching back some fifteen years and extending to the very moment the play proper begins. Here is the history the actors devised.

Early in the marriage, living in London, Richard and Sarah had a marvelous time together; their sexual relationship was conventional but nevertheless satisfying. From her sophisticated women friends, how-ever, Sarah learned of less conventional sex: experiments, different po-sitions, styles. A dyed-in-the-wool conservative, Richard resisted her proposals that they "change" (the very word he will use in his final line). As he informed her, he felt "silly and self-conscious doing . . . you know what." And so six years ago they hit on a plan: loving and faithful to each other, they would impersonate their own lovers, finding their wished-for sexual opposite through a charade. Their sex life would be spiced up, and adultery avoided. By agreement, then, Max-Richard ar-rives every afternoon at three, the precise time the only concession to the scheduled-driven Richard, the length of Max's stay, albeit limited to six when Richard returns, determined only by the nature of their passion at any given session. For five years the game has worked, and then the most curious thing happens: Richard begins to be envious of Max, jealous of his other self! His vanity keeps him from talking hon-estly to Sarah about this change of heart. Significantly, the woman here has no problem with such role-playing; or, as my actress concluded during out table work, if Sarah does have a problem, she is better able to keep her doubts hidden. *The Lover*, then, becomes the unraveling of Richard's desire to end the game, the exposure of what for the last year has been painful and subtextual.

In this light, that short opening scene takes on new meaning, and doubly so. Not only are the characters pretending to have an arrangement with people outside the marriage but Richard, and perhaps Sarah to some degree, wants to end his role as Max, to "kill off" his character. We therefore played the scene in this fashion.

Sarah sat stage right on a divan, wearing a frumpy housecoat; we decided to go a bit further than Pinter's "crisp, demure dress." Pretending to read the newspaper, all the while she eyes Richard who has just emerged from the bedroom, stage left, wearing a formal, British businessman's pin-striped suit. By the upstage-right door, his briefcase and umbrella rest at the foot of a hat rack holding his London Fog raincoat. The routine is for him to ask Sarah with an indifferent look, "Is your lover coming today?" That is, no "amiably" as Pinter calls for on this day which will lead to the unmasking. Today, not hearing or seeing his normal indifference, Sarah suspects that something is about, and in place of her routine "Yes," she replies instead with a quizzical "mmnn," with a subtext of: "why that 'amiable' tone? You've never done that before." Then Richard begins in earnest breaking the rules of the game which dictate that, normally, after her "yes" he cross over, kiss her demurely on the cheek, cross back to the hat rack, put on his coat, pick up the briefcase and umbrella, and toss a "bye-bye" as he leaves. Normally the couple purposely underplay his leaving "ceremony," establishing the personalities of dull husband and bored wife, which only makes the lover's coming that much more exciting.

Today, however, Richard asks a question never asked before, one violating the rules. He inquires about the time; Sarah's "three" therefore had a not-so-subtle subtext of: "you know it's three; it's always three. What is going on?" Now, the otherwise unflappable Richard becomes "flapped," for crossing to her with his "Will you be going out . . . or staying in," he tries to send her a signal: "please say you are going out! If you're at the exhibition, you won't be able to do any passionate lovemaking." Annoyed that he is stepping outside the agreed-upon limits, Sarah now toys with him, first conceding that yesterday she said they would go out, then informing him that she has changed her mind: today she would "prefer" to stay in. As he crosses back to stage center trying to hide his irritation, Richard, usually fluid with words, can offer up only a "mmnn-hmmm," a hurried attempt to appear nonchalant. Visions of steamy sex in his head, hoping that during his cross to the hat rack she will say something, possibly change her mind, or—hope of all hopes!—that she will suddenly reject Max, he suffers through her silence. Our Sarah simply went back to reading the paper. Clearly losing this first round, Richard almost exposes his agony with, "Will he be staying long, do you think?" Turning the knife in him, angry that he has broken the rules, Sarah offers the third "mmnn" of the little scene, this time rich with sexual suggestiveness: it will be a three-hour encounter, enhanced by Max's staying power. As he puts on his coat, Richard reaffirms the time ("about . . . six then"), leaving space in the pause for Sarah to say "four" or "five." He is confronted instead with her firm "Yes." All that he can manage is a cliché, one no sooner said then regretted: "Have a pleasant afternoon." As he picks up his umbrella and briefcase, my Richard on "pleasant" put a little touch of: "Well, then, to your sexual pleasure, not that it bothers me, although I do think that three hours is a bit much." Sarah's final "mmnn" was clearly a "You bet I will." Today, Richard's exit line, "Bye-bye," the standard line from their game plan, is said brusquely, the second syllable almost delivered offstage—he is *that* eager to leave.

The Move Toward "Change"

Decisions made about Richard and Sarah in this first scene chart the course for the rest of the play. This is certainly true for Richard's return from London in the second scene. Even with the audience not yet knowing their secret, how Richard enters, how he accepts the drink offered by Sarah, even the standard kiss on the cheek will reflect just how seriously both characters have taken his violation of the rules in the morning scene. The degree to which Sarah has earlier sensed his dissatisfaction on learning that the plans to go out with the lover have been altered colors her solicitude when he returns from work: "Tired? . . . bad traffic?" Is her "It seemed to me you were just a little late" judgmental? He is supposed to return at six; if Richard is anything, he is punctual. Is it concerned? Perhaps he was victimized by slow traffic? He may be late because he is upset with her, with the arrangement. Or possibly he is trying to change those rigid patterns of his life that make him seem so much less interesting than the unpredictable Max. Its factual basis hidden until Max actually appears, this option can be at best dimly felt by the audience. Our Richard decided to meet Sarah halfway on the issue of traffic. Having corrected her by pointing out that the traffic was "quite good . . . actually," he now concedes, "There was a bit of a jam on the bridge." In rehearsals our reading of this moment was that, whatever their difficulties, difficulties compounded by Richard's and perhaps Sarah's reluctance to come right out with it, they still love each other, are willing to compromise statements or positions.

Still, their paths toward reconciliation or "change" are tortuous ones. Sarah's description of the afternoon as "quite marvelous" annoys Richard, setting the couple back. When he asks her if she showed her lover the hollyhocks, Richard tries to hide a bruised male ego, the subtext being: "just to show you I'm not bothered by your having a 'marvelous' afternoon with your lover, I can be magnanimous by asking if you showed him the same flowers that you and I once took such pleasure in planting." Our Sarah saw right through his fake indifference, qualifying the recollection that her lover was interested in gardening with "Not all that interested, actually": that is, he had better things to do than look at flowers. Her rejoinder reduces Richard to an inarticulate, "Ah"; our Richard made a quick cross to the bar to refresh his drink. There then occurs one of Pinter's famous pauses; the play has over a hundred.

PLAYING PAUSES AND SILENCES

If subtext is at the very least as important as dialogue in Pinter, the pause's silence is equally so. Now the reasons characters go into a pause are numerous. Sometimes it is to "reload," having failed to achieve their object in the line before the pause. Or rendered almost speechless by a partner's witty or sarcastic retort, a character retreats into silence and then tries to recapture the initiative, to get back on the winning side with dialogue after the pause.

Here, Richard's re-entry is only half successful. He changes the topic but only with a recycled question: "Did you get out at all, or did you stay in?" Sarah's firm "We stayed in" again reduces him to a single "Ah." At this point Richard rose from his chair and crossed down to imaginary blinds downstage right. My Lighting Designer gave the illusion in that area of five horizontal lines of light making their way through half-closed slats. With that cross also serving as a pause, Richard, coming out of it, leaps to a new topic: Sarah and her lover haven't opened the blinds after their lovemaking. Sarah herself has failed to observe one of the rules of the game: when Richard returns at six, the room is to be in the same order as when he left in the morning, no matter what happened there from three to six. Actually, Sarah fails twice for she has also not taken off the high-heeled shoes she wears during her trysts. It will be several minutes, though, before Richard spots the error and rather petulantly corrects her.

At other times, one character initiates a pause while the other comes out of that same pause. After telling him that she sometimes, "only at . . . certain times," has a picture in her mind of Richard as she makes love, that it renders the act all the more "piquant," Sarah reassures him that whatever happens with the lover she doesn't forget him. Taken aback, our Richard slumped in his chair; "she does love me," he was saying silently to himself as he fell into a pause after thanking her: "That's rather touching, I must admit." But it is Sarah who brings them out of the pause with what at first seems a demeaning practical qualification: how can she forget him since she's in his house? And then, after Richard caustically reminds her that it is "with another," she drops something of a bombshell: "But it's you I love." This drives both into a pause, one whose silence announces both husband and wife have concluded that, at present, they can go no further. Richard brings them both out of the pause with the suggestion they "have another drink," although this leads, ironically, to his noticing that Sarah still wears high heels as she crosses to the bar.

We spent several of our rehearsals just "playing pauses," that is, the two actors, facing each other, saying out loud what they imagined each of their characters was not saying during the pause. In this way we were rehearsing the play that is almost there. Besides clarifying a character's object during the pause, sharing these otherwise unvoiced lines also allowed each to strengthen that part of their relationship grounded on a deep mutual love.

Knowing the "text" of each other's pauses allowed my Sarah and Richard to establish that same bedrock of love, of trust, that, even with the best of their intentions, the game of their arrangement has obscured. In fact, for a fleeting moment Richard almost uncovers this bedrock when, distinguishing between Sarah and his mistress, he admits that with the latter, "I wasn't looking for a woman I could respect, as you, who I could admire and love, as I do you" (10). Fleeting, because within a few lines they fall to arguing about who cheated first.

THE MILKMAN AND MAX

Many spectators thought that the Milkman was indeed the lover, that Pinter had merely dramatized the clichéd situation of the housewife who, the husband away at work, has an affair with the milkman, or butler, or gardener. We tried to foster this misconception. When the doorbell rang, Sarah struck a sensual pose on the divan as if she were expecting her lover, looking to stage right so as to allow him to sneak up and surprise her. On entering, our Milkman, leering at the body seductively stretched out before him, was barely able to get out his first word, "Cream?" to which audiences invariably supplied their own double-entendres. Still not facing him, Sarah replied with a coy, "You're very late," and it wasn't until she turned on his second "Cream?" that she realized the caller wasn't Max. Still aroused, our Milkman wasn't to be put off. With another leer he told her that "Mrs. Owen just had three jars," and then added what he thought would be a decisive argument for her accommodating him: "Clotted." Once more rejected, he tried a final time with his exit line, "Don't you fancy any cream? Mrs. Owen had three jars."

A vignette of the worst double-entendres, a potentially extramarital cliché denied, the episode with the Milkman served as something of a comic overture for Max's appearance. The majority of the audiences, although they may have had an inkling, didn't suspect that Richard was Max. His entrance always set off a rush of surprised faces, an exchange of knowing looks. Unlike novels, of course, one can't put a play down to reflect on the previous chapter, or even thumb back through the pages to reread a passage in the light of what one now knows. The secret out, I wondered if our audiences found any time to revisit the play so far, to reread that subtext we had so carefully tried to establish. Would the audience be able to think back on that weasel now that it had come out from under the whiskey cabinet?

The Max episode is really two little scenes. In the first, the game they play, where Max as the stranger picks up a married woman in the park, is just that, a lovers' game, the sort of thing one reads about in articles with titles like "Ten Ways to Jazz Up Your Sex Life" or "Game Playing: An Inexpensive Aphrodisiac." Clearly, it has none of the depth of that earlier game played by Richard and Sarah as their real selves.

The little scene 2 is signaled by a quick fade down and up of the lights. Feeling more secure as Max to speak of his wanting to abandon the arrangement, Richard brings to the surface all his subtextual desires, anxieties, and wishes of the play's first half, even inventing children to buttress his argument to stop the game: "My children. My wife's children. Any minute now they'll be out of boarding school. I've got to think of them" (19). No less secure as Delores, Sarah argues for continuing just as they are. Max "wins" on a technicality, claiming she is too thin, that he prefers "enormous women. Like bullocks with udders. Vast great uddered bullocks" (20). In effect, Max and Delores are killed off by an issue of body mass. The game that had sustained their marriage and then plagued it is abandoned.

My actors and I thought of the two scenes with Max as somehow separate from the rest of *The Lover*, necessary to unveil the secret that has been festering from the opening scene up to and including the Milkman's appearance, yet as conventional as the earlier play is unconventional. I purposely rehearsed the Max episode separately, even alternating its rehearsal dates with the rest of the play.

Pinter's "Act 3"

The audience becomes a factor in Pinter's "Act 3," the scene after Max's exit. His exit line, in fact, sets the tone for Richard's return from a day's work: "It's no joke" (20). As my Sarah pointed out, "We [the two actors] don't have to work so hard now, don't need to struggle as we had to when keeping the subtext of the secret beneath the subtext of Richard's jealousy over Max." The audience is now fully in on the joke: when the couple refer to Sarah's lover or Richard's mistress who now "gets thinner every day" we know what they know. Only a tissue of translation now separates a line from its literal meaning, as when Richard suggests Sarah meet her lover in a "field, or ditch, slag heap, or rubbish dump" but no longer in their house (23). Now Richard has no need to separate himself from Max, but can merge the two characters. Cornering Sarah at the upstage-left table, he picks up the bongo drum and, borrowing Max's dialogue from the pickup in the park, with Sarah's help takes off his proper British jacket. Richard's final line, "You lovely whore," announced this healthy merging of mind and body, Richard and Max, Sarah and Delores.

The Lover, I think, has it both ways: it takes a play to celebrate roleplaying as a means to finding one's real self. That real self becomes problematic in Pinter's *A Kind of Alaska*, where the source is not a self-imposed game but an all-too-real medical case history, acknowledged by the playwright in his (atypical) introduction and then enacted onstage.

"Erupt[ing] into Life Once More"

Appropriately, the first performance of *A Kind of Alaska* was for my university's Arts in Medicine Program, which brings artists into the hospital not as entertainers but as collaborators with the healthcare staff.[3] AIM's principle is that artists have much to say about physical and mental health. Our audience that opening night were doctors and staff from the university's Shands Teaching Hospital.

A Kind of Alaska was inspired by *Awakenings*, Dr. Oliver Sacks's account of patients afflicted with *encephalitis lethargica*, or the "sleeping sickness" that spread over Europe in the winter of 1916–1917, and his attempts to bring them out of a their comas by injections of the drug L-DOPA. Pinter focuses on one such patient, Rose (Deborah in the play) who was awoken or, as the playwright describes the transition in his introduction, "erupted into life once more" after a twenty-nine-year coma during which she could hear and see the world about her but could not speak or move without assistance.

I recast the actor who played Richard in *The Lover* as Hornby, Deborah's physician. Accustomed to the challenge of playing the subtext in *The Lover*, he confessed early in rehearsals that he now sometimes felt like "nothing more than a straight man" next to Deborah. That objection would vanish once he discovered the complexity of Hornby's character. Pinter adds a curious love triangle to Sacks's account: Hornby has married Deborah's sister Pauline but, as we played it, has also fallen in love with his patient. More than that, this fairly straightlaced, unimaginative physician envies Deborah: she has had an experience denied him, those years in the coma where, cut off from the outside world, she "lived" in an intense world of the self, an imaginative realm that she spends much of the play trying to convey to this straight man. Still, it is Hornby, however unimaginative, who gives the play its title. Contrasting Deborah in the relative security of the coma, where she has been "nowhere, absent, indifferent," with Pauline and himself, "who have suffered," he tells Deborah that her mind has been "suspended, that it took up a temporary habitation . . . in a kind of Alaska" (Pinter 1982, 34). It is her voyage into this "remote . . . utterly foreign . . . territory" setting her apart that has intrigued him and perhaps made his life with Pauline seem comparatively boring. My Hornby brightened at this project. "I'm the reader who wants to be a poet," was his take, to which I added, "the audience member who wishes he were an actor onstage."

That last analogy was not picked out of the blue, but reflected a translation of the play's opening. I imagined Deborah's bed to be her stage, her performing area, with the audience, first Hornby and later Pauline, in the two chairs called for by the playwright. We put the bed upstage left and the chairs downstage right and close to the first row of the house, at a sharp angle to each other, so that from the house the stage very much looked like an intimate theatre. The blue wash of the general stage lighting contrasted with an amber glow highlighting the bed, and whenever Deborah left the bed, such as when she tries to get up on her own or later dances, her movements were similarly highlighted by pin-spots. For the opening, I also had in mind Beckett's *Not I*, where the loquacious woman, Mouth, upstage left, addresses an Auditor downstage center, who does not speak but only shrugs four times in agreement.

The mood we established in the opening section (5–6) was that of an audience member trying to connect with a performer. "Do you know who I am?" the physician's typical attempt to measure the degree of his patient's consciousness, was for us curiously self-referential: Hornby needs Deborah; his identity is dependent on her. Thus Pinter complicates the doctor's normally superior relation to the patient. This audience of one needs the actor, no less than the actor needs the audience. And if the rule is the patient falls in love with the doctor, here the exception happens: after telling Deborah that he has "married" her sister, Hornby calls her a "widow," confessing that he has "lived" instead with his patient (35). The language with which he describes caring for her is that of a lover: "Some wanted to bury you. I forbade it. I have nourished you, watched over you, for all this time" (34).

The Text as Subtext

There are some relatively conventional moments in *A Kind of Alaska*: Hornby's questioning of his patient, Pauline's appearance, the marital tension between the married couple, the discussion about Deborah's birthday party, Pauline's account of the day her sister fell into a coma, and Hornby's chronicle of the past twenty-nine years of Deborah's life. These moments, however, are overwhelmed by Deborah's descent into deeper and deeper subtextual levels of her life during the coma, which she likens to "dancing in very narrow spaces" (24). Until today buried and hence subtextual in the most literal sense of the term, her dialogue is now present and graphically so. My Deborah thought of her object as a race against time to give expression to this world only she alone has known for twenty-nine years.

Complicating her object is the fact that her onstage audience is not impartial. Hornby is at once enamored and jealous of her; nor, for reasons of his own sanity, does he want to admit that her buried world is more profound than, or imaginatively superior to, presence and consciousness. Male ego notwithstanding, he needs to believe that he has rescued Deborah, a need intensified by his love for his patient. Hornby is like the physician who, seeing death as his enemy, will not let his patient die, despite the patient's wish to do so.

Pauline is clearly overprotective, even going so far as to lie about the family's history during her sister's absence. Complicating her role as audience is the fact that, sensing Hornby's interest in her sister, she sees her as a rival.

My Deborah observed, "I sometimes think that the only people who can understand me are the audience, but I cannot acknowledge them, and they can't speak to me . . . it's frustrating. It's like giving a speech in the dark and hoping against hope that someone is listening." Her remark about not being able to acknowledge the audience would influence a decision I made about the end of the play.

There is a definite progression in the publishing of Deborah's subtextual language. Each moment of consciousness, every interaction with Hornby and then Pauline, drives her deeper into the coma's progressively articulated world.

At first she regresses to childhood and her teenage years, offering the sort of pre-play "history" that an actor would be glad to have as he or she builds the character. I always ask each actor to give his or her character's life story whose latest events, of course, are the play itself. Pinter's dialogue aids Deborah in establishing just such a history as she tells of playing with balloons with her father, of her mother's waking her up in her bedroom with "blue lilac on the walls" (11), her sister Estelle's borrowing her dress. She offers sketches of family members: Estelle's crush on the "ginger boy" from Townley Street (10), Pauline's witty tongue that she predicts will get her in trouble, her own feelings for her boyfriend Jack, rumors about her father's mistress, regret at her mother's not coming to tuck her into bed.

This pre-play history is especially vital to the actress playing Deborah. Physically a middle-aged woman yet stunted in her social development since she has not interacted with others for twenty-nine years, she still has the mentality of a young girl. As she tries to bring this youthful personality into the present, she treats Hornby with a mixture of deference and the arrogance of a young person confronted by a stuffy adult. One moment she fears he has molested her while she was asleep, another that she has been too sexually bold with him; the next moment she is like a child, needing his assurance, plying him with questions. All the time she moves in and out of the present. It is as if the play, confined to the present, were opening up to admit the entire life span of its central character, as if the incident on which Pinter chose to concentrate, the moment of Deborah's awakening, must coexist with the entire life story of Rose in Sacks's case history.

Just before Pauline's entrance, Deborah moves into a second and more profound stage, one whose language is noticeably more poetic. The rather ordinary facts of family life give way to a nightmarish picture of her greedy sister's eating chocolate without taking off the paper wrappers, the chocolate stored for years on the shelves now covered with "ratshit." The memory drives her to a confession: she has wished she "would see no-one ever again," that she could escape "all that eating, all that wit" (18). Hornby's mundane reaction, "I didn't know you had any brothers" (18), which prompts an uncomprehending "What?" from Deborah, seems irrelevant to that rich psychological picture his patient has drawn.

Then, stimulated by Hornby's most detailed account of her condition, one he defines as "neither asleep nor awake" (22), Deborah "eases herself out of the bed" and moves toward him. In our production, her stage, lit in amber, now expanded from the upstage-left bed to center stage as, no longer a middle-aged woman remembering her past, she becomes a young woman, perhaps in her twenties, dancing by herself, playing a guest at a party, converting Hornby to her host: "Any chance of a dry sherry?" (24). Predictably, his second attempt to enter her imaginative world is awkward, halfhearted. Not tied to his facts, comparing herself to Lewis Carroll's Alice, Deborah speaks of "dancing in very narrow spaces," an image she expands to one of threatening psychological proportions: she has lived in "the most crushing spaces . . . the most punishing" (25), burdened by a clumsy dancing partner with a heavy foot. But when the burden is lifted, if just for a moment, she can see a "light," which in turn frees her body so that she can dance all night and day. While mesmerized by this revelation of her life in the coma, a richly metaphoric existence that stands out in stark contrast to the sterile set onstage, Hornby is also frustrated at being excluded from it, envious of his patient whose life now proves to be much fuller, more exciting than his own.

Pauline's entrance calls an abrupt halt to these revelations. Deborah sees through her sister's fraudulently optimistic picture of the family, and senses the tension between the couple. When Pauline asks Hornby, "Doesn't it matter what I say?" he offers only a brusque "No," and her "Shall I tell her lies or the truth" is met with an indifferent "Both." Our Hornby wanted to be alone with Deborah; he resented Pauline's intrusion. Deborah's private life for which she is now finding a language clashes with the rather ordinary marriage of her physician and sister. On Pinter's stage direction for her to cross to the bed, our Deborah moved quickly, eager to return to her "home" (my actress's word for that part of the set). This time we raised the amber lighting for that area 30 percent, and took off a corresponding amount from the wash on the rest of the stage, a signal for the third stage of Deborah's growing subtextual world.

At first Pauline and then Hornby make desperate attempts to win over Deborah. I thought here of a somewhat parallel situation in Pinter's *Old Times*, where Deeley and Anna, present husband and past roommate, try to win over Kate. Accordingly, we staged this section as something of a battle. First, Pauline offers a detailed account of the family dinner when Deborah lapsed into the coma: she was standing with a vase by the side table, about to put the vase down, her arm stretched towards the table, when she "stopped" (30). Deborah crudely if unintentionally dismisses Pauline's effort to explain the past by turning to Hornby and insisting she "must be an aunt I never met. One of those distant cousins" (31). For us, Deborah was not beyond consciously using her odd behavior to make a point. Laughing at Pauline for putting on weight, calling her "mad" (33), Deborah thereby dismisses her sister. Even Hornby comes to Pauline's rescue, insisting that she has been visiting Deborah regularly.

He then launches his own campaign to win her, to be part of her world, correcting the errors and exaggerations in Pauline's family history, polishing his own image as the faithful physician, even going so far as to brand Pauline a "widow" while telling Deborah that he has "lived" with her (35). Deborah's silence cuts off Hornby as well, as if she were dismissing everything he has just said.

Pauline makes one last attempt to win her sister, to bring her into their world, with the promise of a birthday party. But her frantic attempt to paint a gala occasion is swept away by Deborah's move to the third stage, marked by her flicking her cheek, "as if brushing something from it" (37), a neurotic twitch signaling a call from somewhere deep inside her unconscious, from one of those "foreign territories" described earlier by Hornby.

She tells of being in a room whose walls are closing on her; in the darkness she hears a creature panting. The room metamorphoses to her face, now being shut tight with chains and padlocks. A vice is clamped on the back of her neck. Her eyes stuck in place, she can see only the shadow of the tip of her nose. There are horrible smells, and when she asks her listeners if they too can hear a drip, if someone's left the tap on, their silence makes clear that they cannot enter her world. Then she gives the most graphic picture yet of the coma: she lived in a mansion with a vast series of halls, "enormous interior windows masquerading as walls," a mirror world of glass reflecting on glass, and one incredibly still (38–39).

Our Hornby and Pauline stepped back from the bed, sinking into the downstage-right chairs, silent, unable to comprehend the reality Deborah has inhabited. She even abandons her body, her physical self, dismissing her own face as being "of no consequence."

AN AUDIENCE OF PHYSICIANS

As I mentioned earlier, at the opening night performance of *A Kind of Alaska*, commissioned by the Arts in Medicine Program, our audience were physicians and healthcare professionals. In looking at patients from the artist's perspective, AIM tries to make a contribution to medical knowledge. One might similarly argue that in using Sacks's case history as the inspiration for his play Pinter makes his own contribution.

Surely if they have good sense, directors always learn much from audiences: what works, what doesn't work, where the audience discovers something in the play that actors and directors have overlooked. In my notes pinned on the dressing room mirror the day after each performance, I invariably make some suggestions for refining or improving our work based on this unsolicited "advice" from the house. Most often, spectators will not comment directly, but they do speak by the sounds they make during a performance, by their applause to be sure, but also by their posture, by signs of their boredom no less than their excitement. For me, the audience is both an "actor" and "character" in any production.

Our audience from the hospital had much to tell me and my actors about the play, especially the ending. Propped up in her bed, her head supported by pillows, staring diagonally across at her onstage audience of two, Deborah looked very regal, calm, the nervous flicking of the fingers having stopped. She possessed that confidence, the serenity of a tragic hero, of someone "on top of it," as Stoppard's Rosencrantz likes to imagine himself. Having plumbed the three subtextual stages of her coma, having compared that inner, private reality with the mundane future proffered by her physician and sister, Deborah is finally at peace. In conversations at a reception afterward, the physicians read the moment the same way.

Looking directly at Hornby, Deborah offers a bare-bones summary of what he has said, of all that he can tell her. "You say I have been asleep. You say I am now awake. You say I have not awoken from the dead. You say I was not dreaming then and am not dreaming now. You say I have always been alive and am alive now. You say I am a woman." It is a devastating critique of the limits of the physician's diagnosis. He has "cured" her of *encephalitis lethargica*, brought her out of the coma with L-DOPA, but he knows nothing of her, has not been able to comprehend what she has tried to tell him. In the parlance of the actor, he has not abandoned himself sufficiently to respond to the subtext she has discovered and brought to the surface, a discovery on her part that was painful. Hornby is a conventional physician, an audience of one who has failed to do his part. "Just the sort of dispassionate diagnosis that I try every day to avoid," commented one sensitive doctor.

We overrode Pinter's direction, that she look at Pauline and "then back to Hornby," and instead had Deborah divide her next speech between the two, the first two sentences going to Hornby, the next three to Pauline. "She is a widow. She doesn't go to her ballet classes any more. Mummy and Daddy and Estelle are on a world cruise. They've stopped off in Bangkok. It'll be my birthday soon." She reminds Hornby that she is alert enough in the present to realize the facts of his unhappy marriage; our Deborah put an emphasis on the "is." With a grim humor, she even shares a family secret about Pauline's skipping out on ballet classes. Then, turning to her sister, she dismisses her patronizing attempt to cheer her up with that false account of the family, to "treat her like a patient or a child rather than as an adult person," as a psychiatrist in that opening-night audience called it. Even the birthday party she brands as a ruse.

Finally, she includes Hornby in her "I think I have the matter in proportion." Now in the more conventional sense of the term, my Deborah's subtext for this line was: "I see what you are doing. I'm sorry to have been so hard on you. But you cannot enter my world. You think you have awakened me to what is real, but reality is, after all, a relative term. The life you propose to me may not be that wonderful. I have experienced things you cannot know."

Pinter's *Old Times* again comes to mind here. At that end of that play, Deeley and Anna, the two competitors for Kate, are also reduced to silence, sitting immobile on either side of her. Kate, like Deborah, accuses them of failing to see her real self, of trying out of personal needs to fashion her in their own image. Kate asserts, as does Deborah, the primacy of her person. John Graham-Pole, a brilliant pediatric oncologist and the Director of the Arts in Medicine Program, told me that he often "envies" the world of his youthful patients, not their suffering, to be sure, but rather the fact that, "empathize as I may, I cannot enter their world. I stand as a stranger, outside, not being able to be there with them, and, for this reason, in a way failing them." I also think of that moment in Kafka's short story "The Country Doctor" where, as was the medieval custom, the physician crawls in bed with the patient, so as to feel what he feels and thereby extract the pain.

Given this reading, we had Deborah sit upright in bed for her final two words: "Thank you." The line went right to the audience, as if to say: "thank you for being with me, for listening to me. Thank you for trying to do what the two characters onstage could not do: live in my world, however vicariously. Thank you for making a connection with me during this evening's 'entertainment,' for being a good audience." In speaking directly to the audience, my actress's fear that no one was listening to her was erased.

7

Theater from Reality: Co-Director and Co-Author of *More Letters to the Editor*

In the summer of 1994, I directed the premiere of an original play called *Boston Baked Bean* by Shamrock McShane.[1] What especially intrigued me was the work's proximity to reality. During his tenure as Girls Basketball Coach at a nearby high school, McShane had shared an office with the redneck white Head Coach of the track team and the black Assistant Football Coach. Though very unlike, the track and football coaches had become close friends, commiserating in the salty language one encounters in coaches' offices about the fact that for years the black man had, for obvious racial reasons, never been promoted to Head Football Coach and that they worked at a school where sports was low man on the totem pole. Both had to endure the Athletic Director, an annoying man who, wearing his liberalism on his sleeve, wanted desperately to bond with them. The proverbial fly on the wall, McShane had essentially transcribed the real-life conversations of the three men, as well as their true story. The friends kept their sanity by subtly berating the Athletic Director, until halfway through the season they had to part when the track coach left for a better position at a high school in central Florida. That parting, the climax of McShane's play, was a deeply emotional moment for the two. One of the men came to rehearsals and it was "an eerie feeling," as one of my actors observed, to be watched by the living source of the character. Reality took a turn for the better, by the way, when just before opening night the school officials relented, promoting the black man to Head Football Coach.

Boston Baked Bean was replete with references to places, events, and people known by everyone in the community. The play, in effect, cut very close to the present, to real life, and, as we expected, people came to see it who might not otherwise go to the theater. It was something of a documentary, the dialogue the words of actual people, the playwright there when the real-life events generating the plot of *Boston Baked Bean* occurred. Besides, almost everyone here in "Gator Country," as the University of Florida is called, most often with affection, sometimes not, was interested in sports. I decided to capitalize on this appeal by staging *Boston Baked Bean* not only in theaters but in bars, a city building, and a local prison.

During rehearsals my only concern was that the Athletic Director might take offense at his portrait in McShane's play. With the playwright's blessing, we decided not to play him as a buffoon, but as a well-intentioned fellow who somehow lacked social skills, the sort of guy who wants to be part of the gang but tries too hard, someone without serious faults who still never quite fits in. Then, too, the bond between the two coaches was so intense that to admit a third party would be difficult.

I had one specific worry, however. At one point in the play the two coaches make sarcastic references to the Athletic Director's wife: she is a "wealthy woman" and "crazy." Not wanting to hurt the feelings of the real-life Athletic Director, I asked McShane to send him a copy of the script for his approval. Some days later, I got a call: the Athletic Director was thrilled to be impersonated onstage, asked if he and his wife might have two tickets for one of the performances, but had "just a small request." With hesitation and the utmost grace, he wondered if we could insert a third adjective, "beautiful," in the script. His wife was indeed beautiful. We did so—gladly. The night they came I was sitting behind the couple. The amended dialogue went something like this: "Track Coach: 'Yeah, his wife is wealthy . . . and she's crazy . . . ain't she?' Assistant Football Coach: 'Sure, but she's also one fine-looking woman.'" I saw the real-life couple turn toward each other, both touched by the "fine-looking woman." However true to life, *Boston Baked Bean* had pleased them, and I recalled Prospero, Shakespeare's surrogate in *The Tempest*, saying his that "project . . . was to please."

THE PARABOLIC CURVE

I have in recent years been especially drawn to those plays where the theater makes this parabolic curve back to reality, or where the reverse is no less true. Of course, there is nothing new about this. If not with the actual dialogue, Shakespeare's histories invoke a real-life past, at least as interpreted by those Renaissance historians, Holinshed and Hall, that he consulted. That Shakespeare wrote *Henry VIII* in Stratford during his three years of retirement from the public stage may signal an attempt to put some distance between himself and the last English king. In our age, New York's Living Theatre in the 1940s traded on daily stagings of recent events, a public-works project of FDR's administration that asked playwrights to dramatize the current political scene. During the 1960s I took part in "guerilla theater" where we staged theatrical protests against the Vietnam war in front of draft boards: a parody of the aged General Hershey, the Head of Selective Service who himself had never seen military service; a satire on President Nixon; even gruesome simulations of children being sprayed with napalm. More recently I played Maxwell Perkins in a production called *Marjorie and Max*, based on the letters exchanged by that "editor's editor" at Scribner's and the author Marjorie Kinnan Rawlings.[2] That our audience included a good many writers at a conference lent a certain immediacy to a work based on a real-life correspondence. Even a play like Gurney's *Love Letters*, whose correspondence between two doomed lovers is fictional, has a sense of being real; one audience member thought that the actress and I who played the lovers were reading aloud actual letters we had exchanged offstage![3] Television has brought us the docudrama, where the story relies on the audience's association with real figures, past or present. The word "factoid" has been coined to cover dialogue that the real-life prototypes did not actually say but is close to what they *might* have said, or possibly did say.

That life imitates theater is not in question. Erving Goffman has documented the ways in which our everyday behavior involves principles of acting and performance (Goffman 1957). Stephen Greenblatt has done the same thing for Shakespeare's age in *Renaissance Self-Fashioning*. A major innovation of the Renaissance, he argues, was the belief that to a certain extent we can be authors, playwrights of our own lives, that we can fashion the self we wish to present to the world in a way parallel to an actor's fashioning a character (Greenblatt 1980).

That the theater itself can seem "real" is a related, but more cloudy issue. The playwright Jean Genet resolves the issue, perhaps a bit too neatly for some tastes, when he suggests that the only thing distinguishing life from theater is that in the former we pretend that we are not actors, playing, while in the latter we confess the fact or truth all the time (Genet 1967, 79). This is not just a matter of semantics. If as a father I weep at the sight of Lear carrying onstage his dead daughter Cordelia, those tears are real enough, and may, indeed *do* reflect my feelings about my own daughter. The actor playing Lear might, in turn, have drawn upon feelings for his own real-life child: the parent's greatest fear, that of the child's dying.

It is reported that during the filming of *The Lost Weekend*, that brilliant Hollywood film of the 1940s about an alcoholic facing three days when the bars and liquor stores were closed, the star, Ray Milland, actually became an alcoholic. Whether this is true or not, it does underscore our desire, or at least that of the Hollywood publicist, to integrate art with life. I am not talking about "reality TV," that bastard genre where ten oversexed men and women are deliberately stranded on a desert island, albeit provided with cell phones and an attending physician. Relying on a setup, a fake "event," such efforts are only dimly related to theater and, even worse, have nothing to do with the real world. Still, the fact that audiences for the time being clamor for such shows may inadvertently remind us that the theater is the "most real" of all the art forms: it is actually taking place in space and time, is solid in a way a poem cannot be. Not content with this situation, the theater would go further, becoming inseparable from life itself.

No less, the theater can also trick us in taking what happens for reality. Pirandello's *Six Characters in Search of an Author* seems real enough: after all, we are watching real actors play actors in a company about to go into rehearsals for a play actually written by Pirandello. Years ago I saw a New York production of that play where actors, before the official 8 PM curtain, moved about onstage, quietly chatting with each other. The audience assumed they were only getting ready for the show. When curtain time passed, and as the actors gradually raised their voices to performance level, we realized that the play had been in progress all this time. The director had added this overture to the official opening of Pirandello's play about a director and his actors confronting six people who have escaped from the brain of an author incapable of fleshing out their characters.[4]

DIALOGUE FROM LETTERS

Given this interest in the intersection between theater and reality, I was especially drawn to an invitation by my friend William Eyerly that I serve as co-author and co-director for an anticipated production of *More Letters to the Editor*.[5] The idea was borrowed from a company in Pennsylvania that had staged the original *Letters to the Editor* (Stropnicky 1998). A sort of *Our Town*, their show was based on actual letters to the editor of the local paper over the past 150 years. All the dialogue came from real people expressing in actual letters to the paper's editor their ideas, political philosophies, pet peeves, complaints, passions. The

Pennsylvania company found that the production drew people who usually did not go to the theater. When asked why they attended this particular show, the answer was invariably some variation on: "Well, the words I'm hearing aren't fake from some playwright. But from real people. Like me." The dialogue was delivered onstage by actors, but its source was offstage, from people who had no idea at the time that what they were saying in print would one day be staged. The company in Pennsylvania proved tremendously helpful. Within a week of hearing from them, we decided to launch our own production, retitled *More Letters to the Editor*.

From the start we wanted the show to involve the community, not just during the run but in the pre-planning stages. And so we called together some twenty community leaders from politics, journalism, education, and the arts, soliciting their ideas and help. A former professor in the College of Journalism reminded us that the concept of letters to the editor only started after the turn of the century, and so for comments from citizens before 1900 we would have to extract quotes from news stories, perhaps even supplementing those with extracts from diaries and personal letters. We would learn later that because of cultural differences and, most often, indifference or even hostility from newspaper publishers, until recently African-Americans did not usually send letters to the editor. There was a "black supplement" to the local paper, which had a brief life in the 1920s, and we would find that a rich sources of letters. The advisors also suggested that given the bulk of such letters, we focus on certain historical periods, or issues, instead of conducting a random search for material. For our part, my co-director and I wanted letters that, whatever their inherent merit, would also work as stage dialogue. The relevance of the letters to the daily lives of our projected audience was never in question, but we did need material that would be good for actors.

We knew that the great majority of our letters would come from the town's major newspaper, *The Gainesville Sun*, which over the years had evolved from *The Sun* to the *Morning Sun* to *The Daily Sun*. There was also a paper called *The Bee* or *The Weekly Bee* which preceded the *Sun* in the last century. In addition, we would want to use the student newspaper of the University of Florida, *The Alligator*. We would also consult a variety of cult newspaper, like *Moon* (which covers everything from left-wing politics to the entertainment scene) and *The Iguana* (something of an "underground" newspaper).

Instead of doing a book show like that of the Pennsylvania company, we opted for something closer to a review, a series of related scenes rather than a single story line. Playing the cynical co-authors, we reasoned that a variety of different scenes would keep the audience's attention: "If they don't like this scene, there's always the next," or "you can't hit a moving target." We would divide up the letters and, separately, each write skits, then look at our work and decide on what would go into the show.

The reason here was not entirely one of efficiency or division of labor. My co-director and I knew we would have different approaches to the material. Eyerly was inclined more toward the play format, the skit fashioned like a mini-drama, with characters in the customary sense of that word. Having for four years been Director of Strike Force, an improv group of the University of Florida's Theater Department, I was given to skits closer to vignettes, routines, comedy bits, or, with more serious pieces, skits that set a mood but with less emphasis on the story line. We also agreed that it was essential for the integrity of the show to use only the words from the actual letters. Of course, we would edit letters, cutting them down to size for delivery, using extracts here and there. But we would never add any words of our own. Whenever possible we would also give the date of the letter and the paper in which it appeared.

We were concerned that *More Letters to the Editor* be not just a random collection of skits, and were determined, therefore, to organize the scenes so that they would play off each other, with connections based on motifs, themes, formats, and time periods. This concern proved to be more imaginary than real, for the ultimate force binding the show was the sense of *More Letters*'s being a mirror for a community speaking to itself, voices from past and present witnessed by an audience who shared many of the same concerns, and had, in many cases, written their own letters to the editor.

We decided to use an essentially bare stage, an area where fellow citizens, impersonating various writers to the editorial page over the two centuries, would confront fellow citizens seated in the house. The walls upstage and stage left were covered with newspapers, a choice that was surely appropriate, not to mention economical.

There would also be many moments when actors could play directly to the audience, even perform from the audience. And to enhance this connection between house and stage, we would have as one of our scenes "The Celebrity Guest," where a well-known person in the community would come onstage and read excerpts from actual letters. With the actors playing the guest's fan club, the celebrity from the house would become a temporary part of the performance.

We also tried to establish an informal atmosphere for the production. Once actors were in makeup, they would come onstage before the 8 PM curtain, greet and chat with the audience, or go upstage and sing songs around a piano, like guests at a cocktail party. Nor was there any backstage. When actors finished a scene, they would take seats on stage left, as if they were now just fellow members of the audience; they were further encouraged to react to the performance as any spectator might do. We used blackouts for effects rather than to create any illusion of time passing or scene divisions. Similarly, there were some special-effects lighting, but in general we performed in full stage lighting. As with our decision about the letters themselves, we wanted to strike a balance between content and staging, between our real-life sources and theatrical illusion.

Because an enormous number of people turned out for auditions, we could shape the cast to resemble that cross-section of the community we had sought in both the letters and the staging. Besides fifteen young people, we had in the cast two African-American actors, an Asian-American, a senior citizen, and men and women ages nineteen to forty-five.

Rehearsals were challenging in that the actors were asked to delve into the subtext or history of the real-life people who had written the letters, without being able to stay in character for the full length of the play. Because the nine actors appeared in many scenes, playing many parts, they had to establish characters quickly, without recourse to previous scenes, not to mention dialogue from the mind of a single playwright. Much of the acting involved ensemble work, intricate timing, split-second changes; some of it was fairly physical. *More Letters* was, to say the least, a somewhat "new" experience for the actors accustomed to a single play by a single playwright.

THE SCENES

There were nineteen scenes in *More Letters*. Several of them resembled mini-plays. In "Breakfast with McCarthy, Smith, and Wesson" a gathering of the generic American family turns serious when the father reads a letter from a 1960s paper about a fifteen year-old schoolboy who shot himself with a 32-caliber pistol. After the husband leaves for work, the wife reflects a moment on the tragedy but then is diverted by an ad in the paper for laundry detergent. In "The Quilting Bee" five women sit in a circle reflecting on a variety of topics coming from letters to the editor published between 1882 and 1884. By exerting financial and marital pressure on their husbands, they conclude that even without the right to vote, they still control local elections.

Many of the scenes were looser in structure. In "The Angry Crowd" the actors played various people writing complaint letters, on every topic from drunks at football games to the firing of the school superintendent. As the tone became more frantic, the actors "melded" to the stage, a mass of writhing, angry bodies, relieved only by strains of John Lennon's "Imagine" which, once they were calmed, led to a single topic on which all could agree: "Go Gators!" the chant for the university's football team. In "The Circle" men and woman voiced opinions about women's rights, using writers from 1880 to 1975. The two sexes soon fell into warring camps, men and women moving about like boxers sparring, with hostilities ceasing when one of the actresses began singing Helen Reddy's "I Am Woman" as her sisters who had joined her asked now-chastened men to sing with them.

Most often the scenes offered a collage of views on a single topic. In "The Early Gainesville: 1883–1898" actors would come running onstage, deliver a letter, then rush off with the next actor following right behind. They assaulted the audience with commentary on everything from building a new train line through the area to a citywide quarantine for yellow fever. "Letters from Abroad" featured soldiers from the two world wars writing to parents and loved ones. As a narrator made his way among various stations onstage, the writers would come alive. We interspersed the comments with popular war songs such as "I'll Be Home for Christmas" and "The Last Time I Saw Paris." Similar in format was "Why Do I Feel so Black and Blue?" composed of letters from racists to those of civil rights leaders about African-Americans, from 1903 to the present. Again, a narrator "activated" actors at various stations onstage; she tied the segments together with the song "Why Do I Feel So Black and Blue?" from the musical *Ain't Misbehavin'*. One of these letters, charging the university's Theater Department with racial discrimination, was actually written by the actress playing the narrator, and while we did not identify her (nor any of the letter writers), at this point the play came as close to reality as possible. In "Voices of the Future" the young actors of the company delivered letters they would like to write to the local paper, asking the audience not to reject them because of their age, to "listen" to them. The topics were a mixture of the silly (a tax on Pac Man addicts) to the serious (drugs, child molesting).

Four scenes were based on actor's games and television shows. In

"Word Games with Letters" the actors impersonated automobiles, their drivers speeding across the stage with a host of clichés from letters complaining about Gainesville traffic, while in "Angry Words" the young actors went through the acting exercise "The Alphabet," where they sped through the alphabet using buzzwords from recent letters to the editor. In "School" a harassed teacher wrote down on a blackboard words shouted to him by unruly students calling out everything from "educationalize," "magnet schools," or "mandatory uniforms," to hot topics like affirmative action and neighborhood schools. We even had "A Letter Bake-Off" with an unctuous emcee and four contestants; the winner was the one who could say ten words or phrases on a given topic in the shortest amount of time. Those topics were: "Life in Gainesville," "Gun Control, "Money," and "Local Politics."

We also had various monologues, some delivered by a single actor center stage, others put in a dramatic context. "Women-Right" featured a conservative male in 1925 attacking "uppity women," while in "Going to the Dogs," after complaining to his wife about a neighbor's dog who bit him as he was bending down to pick up the morning paper, the writer offered a simple plan to deal with "pesky animals"—death. He equated anyone opposing his plan with the Communists. In "Oliver Park" an actor impersonated a man in 1883 annoyed by young women using the park without a chaperon; he was answered by an actress insisting that women had the right "to go by themselves." "A Matrimonial Ad" appeared in a 1865 paper where a male writer objected to a young woman who had placed an ad seeking a husband. "Fonda and Baez" came from a former colleague of mine who in 1971 castigated the two popular entertainers for using a campus visit to push their anti-Vietnam war views. "Town Meeting: Impeachment" was a crowd scene where the speaker in 1974, a local politician, pleaded with the voters not to push for the impeachment of President Nixon. Unable to convince the mob, he acceded to their wishes because they had "elected him as their representative." Holding his hands before the voters in a manner reminiscent of Pontius Pilate, he declares, "I wash my hands of any responsibility for what follows."

We had several strategies in the arrangement of scenes. Trips back to the last century were juxtaposed with letters from papers as recent as the present year. Mini-plays were followed by "mood" pieces. Monologues were mixed with fairly elaborate production numbers that included music and narrators. The topics ranged from the trivial to the deadly serious. A comic scene might suddenly become tragic. We tried to represent all voices, especially those of minorities; conservative viewpoints shared the stage with liberal counterarguments. We tried not to push any single agenda. While the letters spoke for themselves, the actors also discovered a subtext of which the writer was sometimes unaware or, at best, only partially aware.

AUDIENCE REACTION

More Letters to the Editor played to almost full houses for five weeks. In fact, we had taken something of a gamble with the run, scheduling three weeks before the December holidays break and then re-staging the play for two weeks in January. Fortunately, word of mouth did its job and, if anything, the theater was even more full during those final two weeks. As we anticipated, the audience's reaction was different from that normally accorded a "straight" play. The literally hundreds of references to local personalities and events hit home; standing in the back of the theater I could see couples turn to each other, exchanging knowing looks at the mention of someone they liked or disliked. As one audience member put it, there was a "comfort" in hearing the name of a local store or street, or the latest burning issue, whether it be high gas prices in a college town or the planning board's recommendation to replace four-way stop streets with traffic circles. Some issues led to especially intense audience reactions, particularly women's rights and racial problems. Everyone sat glued to the final skit as the young actors voiced their concerns; I suspect some of the audience anticipated the teenagers would shy away from serious topics. The mood in the theater was relaxed, informal, and while we had done much to encourage this, it also sprang from the nature of the show itself. "Like a town meeting" was one friend's tag for the evening.

In April, three months after the show closed at the Acrosstown, we took it on tour, thanks to a grant from the Florida Humanities Council. We played at five locations in Gainesville, including a city building, a recreational center, the library, and a retirement center. We also traveled to three locations in small towns outside the city: a community theater in Chiefland, the Women's Club in Alachua, and a music hall atop a restaurant/gift store in High Springs.

The Humanities Council had funded the tour so that we could use *More Letters* as a springboard for post-play discussion with the audience. To allow room for that discussion, and yet to keep the running time within reasonable limits, we took an abridged version on tour, eliminating the monologues, some scenes whose issues were anticipated elsewhere, and, in a few cases, scenes that had not worked quite as well as others. For the discussions, I invited three of my colleagues (from English, Classics, and the Law School) to join me. Typically, after the performance the actors would go offstage and sit with the people in the house. The humanists would then make a few opening observations: placing some of the letters within the larger context of, say, African-American culture or the women's rights movement, or raising ethical and political question about this type of forum, notions of how the theater interacts with reality, even remarks about the prose style or intentions of letter writers. We also used "celebrity guests" for the tour; outside of Gainesville that guest would be someone from the immediate community. Back in Gainesville, the guests were often suggested by audiences who had seen the original production in December or January.

We did invite one celebrity guest back for the tour, Ron Cunningham, the Editor of *The Gainesville Sun*'s editorial page. An obvious choice, he could give all of us an insider's view of his job, and was consequently besieged with questions. What percentage of letters were printed? How representative did he try to be with differing political or religious positions? Are there certain letters that the paper won't print? To what degree does the editor's own bias or agenda influence the choice of letters to include? Except in certain cases, such as a letter from a rape victim, why does the paper insist on giving names with letters?

What was fascinating in these discussions was how quickly the audience got to major questions beyond the letters themselves. Rather than spending much time talking about specific moments in the show or complimenting the actors, the audience generally *used* their immediate experience to approach larger issues. And this is precisely what we wanted. Rather than get into a debate about the sales tax or some unpopular public official, we wanted them to focus on the community itself: how it voices its views? how tolerant are its citizens of minority views? how empowered or un-empowered did the residents feel when exercising their right to speak on the issues? People who were frequent writers of letters spoke as effectively about their "hobby," as one called it, as those who confessed they had never written, or would never write a letter to the editor. There was frequent debates on the value of such letters, the views here ranging from the practice being an exercise in futility or vanity, to a useful psychological release valve, to "the closest thing we have to a democracy."

Cunningham cited an interesting fact: a few years back, his paper took a poll asking readers what section of the paper they turned to first.

The answer was not the sports page, as many of us might expect, but letters to the editor. As the audience extrapolated from the letters we had used to the larger issue of putting our private thoughts in print, it was clear that most of them were avid readers of this section of the paper. An English professor, I was especially intrigued with comments about the "paradox" of letter writing. After all, a letter can be an intimate form of expression, yet the writer to the editorial page clearly knows, indeed *expects* that such private thoughts will be made public, and with the writer's name attached. For me, the letter to the editor thus steers between our private and public worlds. Not even the writer's subtext could escape the scrutiny of the actors of *More Letters to the Editor* and, it is hoped, the awareness of the audience.

My co-director and I were profoundly affected by the experience of collaboration: workshopping with the actors this play made from scratch, exploring the interface between reality and the theater. Perhaps most important, we had the opportunity to use the theater not just as "entertainment" (in the most limited sense of that word), but as part of our public, democratic dialogue. And, I must add, we had the opportunity of playing before people who had never entered the theater before.

8

Playing the House

ACTORS KNOW OF COURSE, THE AUDIENCE IS OUT THERE IN THE house; the audience knows the actors know this—*ad infinitum*. Two groups, two explorers, if you will, charting the same territory yet acting as if they were unaware of each other's presence. "A conspiracy," as an actor-friend calls it. They are the two halves of an equation that constitute a performance, and both actors and audience have vital roles to play. As a veteran actor once told me when I was starting out in the business, actors playing to an empty house are just in rehearsal, and people sitting looking at an empty stage are not an audience. It takes two.

The veteran actor's reminder that audience and actor need each other was his way of scolding me when I complained that our audience, wealthy main-line Philadelphians, came just because "it [was] fashionable" and for this reason were "unworthy" of us. He grabbed me by the ear, and told me in a gruff voice, "They're your audience, and never forget that. Whether they're bright or stupid, sober or drunk, they're still your audience. You need them; you're playing *for* them. So stop complaining!" Indeed, actors play for an audience, make a play for them, literally and figuratively. There are things directors can do to engage that audience.

THE CIRCLE OF THE AUDIENCE

A few years back, I directed a college production of Wendy Wasserstein's *Uncommon Women and Others* that, given the circumstances, made a parabolic curve from the stage back to reality.[1] After all, I was staging this play about women from Wellesley College facing graduation before an overwhelmingly undergraduate audience. What could be more relevant, or closer to the reality just offstage? To up the stakes, I had the then-President of the University of Florida, John Lombardi,

107

do the voice-overs that precede each act. Wasserstein uses the actual inaugural address of the first male president of Wellesley. I even gave our 1990s audience a little "history lesson," prefacing the show with a short skit set in a college dorm, where two women in the course of a conversation squeezed in all the play's references to terms, personalities, and events peculiar to the 1970s. When *Uncommon Women* started, my young audience, all born in the 1980s, would thereby have a form of *Cliff Notes* for the performance. "Why don't you just start the play where Wasserstein starts the play?" a colleague demanded. I could not fully justify what I did; I only know that I wanted my audience to have some orientation for what must otherwise have seemed to them a "quaint," somewhat remote world.

But the most important decision was to do the play in the round, a choice that invariably complicated the blocking but was designed to give the audience the sense of being one of the many concentric circles suggested by Wasserstein's own text: the all-female cast playing women who have bonded during their four years, now facing anxieties about leaving the protective womb of their college campus, and moving out into the larger circle of a world dominated by men. While there are no men in the cast itself, the women make numerous references to boyfriends, fathers, male authority figures, all just off-campus. Surrounding the stage on all sides, seeing fellow audience members across the stage, the audience itself formed a final circle, outside the smaller, illusory circles of the play's world.

Surely there are limits to involving the audience. "I can just sit there, right? You won't bring me up onstage?" one audience member at the opening of *Boys in the Band* asked me at the theater door, knowing that in the 1960s I was very much into participatory theater, dragging audience members onstage, breaking down the barrier between the stage and the house.[2] "No, that was years ago and I've changed," I replied, and this reassured him. But I do recall an Oklahoma production of *Hamlet* in the round where the audience was not allowed to sit passively in their seats.[3] There were three separate stages forming a half circle, with the audience seated on swivel chairs. Three separate casts performed Shakespeare's play, with the performance switching from one stage to another according to the director's concept. On stage one was the neurotic, dark, brooding Hamlet, one just an inch away from a mental institution; on stage two was the bright Renaissance prince, martyred by the Gestapos of Claudius's court; stage three was Ernest Jones's Oedipal Hamlet, awash in formative teenage sexuality, lusting after Gertrude, insanely jealous of Claudius's intimacy with his mother!

The production moved from one *Hamlet* to the next, not just between scenes, but within scenes, even in the middle of speeches, or individual lines. I cannot remember anything about the performance itself, or rather the *performances*, except rotating back and forth in those swivel chairs, and thinking that this was just a bit too much involvement.

I recalled this experience years later when I did *Hamlet*.[4] We staged it in the round, complete with a circular small stage in the center which doubled as the guard's platform, a sitting area, the performance space for *The Murder of Gonzago*, the grave in 5.1, and the arena in which Hamlet and Laertes dueled. Doing Shakespeare's play in the round gave each spectator an intimate relation with the action; I even let the Clown play the audience. But may the gods be thanked, there were no swivel chairs, let alone three simultaneous *Hamlet*s.

BLURRING THE LINES BETWEEN THE HOUSE AND THE STAGE

I spoke earlier of the involved prison audiences we had for a tour of *Waiting for Godot*. Louis Tyrell, an actor friend who directed a production of Beckett's *Endgame*, had a similar experience. Scheduled for a two-week run in a penthouse theater that was part of a luxury high-rise for wealthy retirees in Tampa, his production had to be canceled after six performances.[5] Despite their successes in life, their comfortable retirement, the well-heeled audience of senior citizen "freaked out" (Tyrell's words) during the performance. Hamm facing death, his own endgame, venting his suffering on his servant Clov, terrified of the young boy who appears outside the window, all this was too much for them. The audience could not separate the onstage story from what they were experiencing, or had experienced in real life. Tyrell was that worried about their physical and mental health. We Americans sometimes wonder about those French, bursting out of the concert hall and rioting in the streets after first hearing Stravinsky's *Rite of Spring*. But clearly the French do not have a monopoly on extreme reactions to a performance.

Audiences, of course, refashion any play in light of their own lives, needs, preoccupations, biases. You never know what to expect. I recall sitting behind two young couples at a production of Pinter's *The Lover* that I had directed.[6] I often do this, sit with the audience, as obscurely as possible, to feel, to measure their reactions. Is this bit of business working? Is that scene playing the way we intended? Audiences will also discover things you never intended, laughing at a line that in rehearsal didn't seem all that funny, latching onto a character who before the opening seemed a minor, even dull figure. The two couples were having a wonderful time. I could sense that early on, before the arrival of Max (the alter-ego of the husband, his wife's "lover"), they had figured out the couple's little secret: Richard, the husband, plays Max. But halfway through this short play the couples got up and quietly made their way out to the lobby. Why were they leaving? What had I done wrong? Weren't they enjoying the show? I raced to the lobby, catching up with them just before they were about to leave the building. Breathless, I asked, "Is something wrong? Don't you want to stay for the rest of the play?" In a polite, sophisticated voice, one of the men replied, "Oh, we *loved* the show. But we've seen as much as we wish to tonight." Somehow a sign atop a local restaurant flashed through my mind: "Ryan's Buffet—'All You Care to Eat!'" There is no accounting for audience taste, or attention span!

That term, audience, covers more than just those paying to see the performance. When I was teaching at the University of Illinois I staged a production of Edward Albee's *Zoo Story* one evening in the courtyard of an apartment complex.[7] In this appropriate setting, with a real bench under real trees, including a fountain gurgling nearby, the sounds from the street helped enhance the illusion that we were watching two real men, the conservative Peter and the neurotic Jerry, during a chance encounter in New York's Central Park. Everything went as normal until the final scene where, forcing Peter to assert himself, Jerry so enrages the otherwise timid man that he stabs him in the chest, all this to "thank yous" from the victim. Just at the climactic moment, two Champaign-Urbana policeman, having heard the commotion, pulled up and burst onto the stage, handcuffing Peter and calling 911 for Jerry. Half laughing at their mistake, half-shocked by their reactions, the audience only drove the two cops to focus more intently on their job. Fortunately, within a few minutes everything was explained away; we all had a good laugh, though, as I recall, as the cops departed one said to his partner something to the effect that this was "just what you'd expect from those theater types."

Three years later, when I was teaching at Boston University I had a second, very different encounter with the audience for a production of *Zoo Story*.[8] After a successful run of the play, I invited my two actors to do it for an evening-school class I was teaching on "Modern Drama." This was an especially good group, whose members had become quite skilled and very articulate in judging performances; as a result, we had many requests from local companies and artists to perform for us.

I introduced the play, and then went to the back of the large class-room to watch my two charges. Jerry approached Peter right on cue with, "I've been to the zoo." Peter "*shrugs*" (Albee 1974, 12), trying to bury himself in the *Times*, ignoring the intruder. But before Jerry could say his second line, "I said I've been to the zoo," my actor froze. He couldn't remember the line, even though he had had much experience in the theater and the line in question was only a slight variation on his opening line. Now, when something like this happens onstage, when an actor forgets a line, there are two alternatives. You can start over, but this, of course, breaks the spell, besides possibly calling attention to the dropped line. Or, with the help of your fellow actor, you can improvise a way back into the dialogue as written. I fully expected my Peter, seeing his partner go blank, to say something like "Did you just say you'd been to the zoo?" Of course, an improvised line like that would ruin Peter's pose of indifference. Jerry, surprisingly, took the first alter-native, stepping backward until he was offstage, re-entering, repeating the first line correctly, getting the shrug from Peter, and then going blank a second time. He looked at me standing at the back of the room; with my hands and eyes I tried to tell him it was OK, that since he had done the play so successfully in the past, I was sure everything would be fine the next time. My plan was to take the two actors aside, perhaps to the next room, go over the opening, and come back. Before I could intervene, however, Jerry tried again, from the top. Once more he for-got that second line. This third time he grabbed his partner and as he hurried toward the door looked at me, his eyes welling in tears, and cried out, "I'm sorry, Sid—I've broken the illusion!"

They left. The class was stunned. I checked: they had gone; the hall was empty. Going back into the classroom I asked my students if they wanted to talk about what had just happened. At first, like lovers after a quarrel, they avoided the topic, talking about everything else but what we had just witnessed. Then, slowly they got around to the subject at hand. It was fascinating that about half the audience thought that what we had just seen was real: that is, we had watched an actor forget his line, become frustrated with each attempt, then bolt for the door. But the other half of the class argued that it was all a setup, that what we had witnessed was a play about an actor forgetting his lines, that none of it was real. As one member of this group pointed out, "We don't say things in life like 'I've broken the illusion'!" She elaborated on her point: there was a vocabulary, a style peculiar to the stage that would be unnatural in real life. Predictably, someone from the other group ar-gued the opposite: not only were the stage and life closer than we think, or assume, but our attendance at this real-life happening had elevated it to the level of theatre. I was reminded of the experiments we tried in New York during the 1960s, assembling as an audience on a street corner, waiting for the first traffic accident, or argument, and believing that our presence somehow "made theater" out of what in life would otherwise be random, and meaningless to everyone but the people involved.

The next day, my student, my Jerry, came to my office hours, hat in hand, saying he wanted "to explain what really happened last night." Now, usually I am eager for facts, for explanations. I had my own theory about what had happened, having silently cast my lot with one of the two student groups in last night's discussion. But this time I violated my own principles, and, in a strange way, like to think I was better for doing so. "No, don't tell me . . . no need to tell me. Let it remain a mystery, unsolved." "But why?" he protested. "Don't you want to know the truth?" "When it comes to the theater," I answered in my best professorial tone, "I sometimes prefer ambiguity to truth."

Spectators and Real Life Readings

The Florida Endowment for the Humanities has funded several of my theatrical productions over the years. Their requirement is that the show serve as a springboard for discussion with the audience, and this requirement has invariably led to assembling specific audiences for specific plays. In turn, such audiences will often bring an agenda to the performance that colors their response which, in turn, influences everything from the choice of plays to the actors' work onstage. I have had grants from the agency for two productions in Florida prisons (*Waiting for Godot* in 1974, and in 1991 a two-hour show of *Saturday Night Live*–style skits, based on issues of concern to the inmates and the prison staff), performances before elderly audiences of David Mamet's *The Duck Variations* in 1979 and *King Lear* in 1998, a program on AIDS with a 1988 performance of *As Is*, and a recent production of *Shakin' the Mess Outta Misery* where a diverse audience was asked to talk about the African-American experience.

It was, however, my first grant from the Florida Humanities Council in 1973–74 that brings back the strongest memories. The production was called *Florida's Madding Crowd*, a collage of scenes from plays about life in the inner city, the suburbs, and the country. Using parts of some nine plays, we looked at the ways in which people preserve their individuality even as they function as members of a larger community. We toured all over the state of Florida, from large cities to small towns. It was our final performance at Miami Dade Community College, in north Miami, which proved most memorable.

Our large audience was a fairly even mixture of college students and senior citizens. We ended the evening with two scenes from Ionesco's play *Rhinoceros*. In the first, the compromising Frenchman Dudard tries to convince the hero, Berenger, to give in to the rhinos who, once a minority, have now seized power in the town. Between the scenes I reminded the audience that Ionesco had fought with the underground during World War II, and that the rhinos, allegorically, were the Nazis, or any vicious group that corrupts a once-civil society. The performance ended with Berenger's monologue which closes Ionesco's play, where he desperately wishes that he could be like everyone else, become a rhinoceros, with a rhino's skin, protruding horn, raucous voice (Ionesco 1989, 105–7). Berenger longs to become one of the beasts, but fails. Then he concludes that since he cannot be a rhino, he is determined to stay a human, even if he is the only human in town.

Afterward, we had discussion with the audience over coffee and doughnuts in a large room adjacent to the stage. One of my actors and I had become wedged into a corner, surrounded by a crowd telling us their favorite scenes, their least favorite scenes, most often making connections between what they had seen on stage and their own lives. Then, from the far corner of the room an elderly couple appeared, a little gray-haired lady tottering on her husband's frail arm. He was wearing a yarmulke. They must have been ninety-five if they were a day. The crowd parted respectfully as they made their way slowly towards us. The old man thanked us for a fine evening, and then his wife added they she especially enjoyed the two scenes from *Rhinoceros*. In my best teacher's style, I asked what in specific about the performance had impressed them. The actor who played Berenger was at my side. "Oh, it wasn't anything you did, sonny," she replied, placing her hand in mine. "It was . . ." and then she hesitated. The old couple looked at each other, communicating with their eyes the way two people who have lived a long life together speak to each other without words. She seemed to be asking her husband's opinion on something, and when he nodded a silent "yes," they both rolled up their sleeves. There, embedded in their upper arms were concentration camp numbers. I burst into tears, as the old woman squeezed my hand and said simply, "It wasn't your fault, sonny."

As we drove home to Gainesville, the long tour over, I thought to myself: imagine how those two precious audience members were receiving the play! How, beyond any conscious effort on our part, they were reweaving the performance into the rich, profound, tragic fabric of their own lives. And how shallow, how uninformed my narrator's remarks about the Nazis or Ionesco's allegory now seemed in comparison to what they had brought to the performance. With the best of intentions, we had indeed played *with* and *for* them. And as our audience, they had played their role well, enriching our performance in ways unfathomable to director and actors.

APPLAUSE FROM A TRAIN

Even inanimate things can serve as an audience and, what is more, applaud and thereby contribute to the production. When I was teaching at the University of Illinois, some of my colleagues and I rented an abandoned train station in downtown Urbana and established the Depot Theatre. The station had once served passengers but now no longer. Every night at 10 PM, though, a noisy freight train would go racing by on its way to southern Illinois. The station would shake and rattle; the deafening noise could go on for four or five minutes. We learned to time our performances so that they would end before ten, and thus avoid interference from the "gross intruder," as we called the freight train. However, one night, at a performance of *The Tempest*,[9] the audience had been especially appreciative, stopping the production several times to applaud. And with a full house, the intermission, normally fifteen minutes, had gone on twice as long. As a result, just as Prospero was beginning his epilogue I could feel, even before I heard it, the freight train approaching from the north. Also aware of the imminent train, the actor playing Prospero speeded up his delivery. Would he get to Shakespeare's final line—"Let your indulgence set me free"—before the gross intruder drowned him out? By some miracle he did! The line delivered, the audience burst into applause. As it went thundering by, for once in its otherwise lonely, mechanical existence, the train, this mere machine enhanced that applause, blending its sound with the audience's clapping. The actors quickly joined Prospero for the curtain call so as to share in this unexpected ovation. Perhaps for the only time in its dreary life of hauling supplies to Carbondale, an inanimate object had known the theater.

9

Different Audiences

I HAVE TAKEN THE THEATER TO THE FLORIDA PRISONS AND TO THE Teenage Psychiatric Ward of Shands Teaching Hospital on the University of Florida campus. But one warning. I will scream the next time someone, with delusions of originality, jokes, "Ah, prisons. Now there's a captive audience!" And one disclaimer: When working with troubled teenagers, I don't consciously use the theater as therapy. For one thing, I have no qualifications to do so; I'm not a psychiatrist, nor even a "healthcare provider," to use the current collect-all term. Nor am I convinced that role-playing provides a magic pipeline to the psyche: life and the theater are not, I think, so interchangeable. The warning and the disclaimer aside, I have played before these two audiences, not your typical audiences, to be sure, but nevertheless audiences that in very special ways both challenge the actor/director and offer reverse mirrors for the stage's world of illusion.

"Why Don't You Come Over and Do That *Endgame* Thing Tomorrow?"

I have mentioned earlier in this book and have written elsewhere more extensively about the experience of staging Beckett's *Waiting for Godot* in the Florida prisons: of how the inmates talked to the actors during the performance, their erasing the boundary between house and stage, and the intense conversations afterward, where each inmate gave a personal response to Godot's identity.[1]

It was the memory of our final performance at Cross City Prison on Florida's Gulf Coast that would stay with me for twenty years and lead to a second, very different tour. Cross City is a medium-security facility. At this stage in the tour, the *Godot* cast was accompanied by numerous students and colleagues, who allowed us to split into small, more manageable discussions after the performance.

That April night our performances took four hours, twice the normal running time, given all the productive interruptions from the audience. There followed a one-hour discussion with the inmates, after which they were taken to their cells in a dormitory on the far side of Cross City's campus-like setting. Following conversation with the Warden and his staff, we were led out of the auditorium and across the prison yard to the main gate. A large contingent of guards escorted us; they were nervous because of riots at the prison the week before. At the opposite end of the yard stood the darkened dormitory where the inmates were housed and, supposedly, had been asleep for an hour.

Just as the gates clanked open, we all heard barred windows being raised from across the yard. Already nervous, the guards got into battle formation, expecting the worst. Then we heard the inmates; they had been waiting up to call out "good-nights" and "see yas" to us. It was nothing more than a sentimental human farewell. The guards shook their heads in disbelief, dismissing the occasion as "what happens when you let weird students and liberal professors visit." We heard our names called out in the darkness—"Good-night, Sid," "See you, Betty!"—and shouted back farewells in response. It was surreal, voices in the night hurtling back and forth across the sterile prison yard, to an audience of sullen guards. Then, we heard a familiar voice of one John, blessed with a distinct Bronx accent.

John was an especially troublesome inmate, always picking fights or leading protests. When you are that troublesome in the Florida system, the authorities respond by moving you from prison to prison, to break up your power or drug connections, along with any friendships you might make in that strange world. John had been so moved four times, and therefore tonight's production of *Godot* was the fourth one he'd seen. John had become a favorite of ours, the cast dubbing him "Our Resident Beckett Expert." Across that black prison yard John's voice boomed out, "Good-night, Sid!" I shot back a "Good-night, John." John followed with a seemingly innocuous question, "Hey, Sid, that Beckett fellow, he wrote another play called *Endgame*, didn't he?" I was thrilled that John, already familiar with *Godot*, knew this second play by Beckett. "Yes, yes, John, he did write *Endgame!*" It was John's response, so simple, so impossible, and, as I would realize, so profound, that stayed with me. "Well, I tell you what, Sid. Why don't you come over and do that *Endgame* thing tomorrow?"

Didn't he know that you didn't just "do" a play, that it took weeks of rehearsal? How could he be so naive about the theater? On the drive back to Gainesville we all raised such obvious questions. Then what he said sunk in. Consider John's notion of the theater. A play is as simple, as basic, takes no more preparation than a conversation between two friends, two people; the one speaking is the actor, the one listening, the audience. And in our prison production of *Godot* those roles had changed hands from house to stage. Understood this way, John was right. A play is as natural, as effortless, as *human* as a conversation. In a way, we could come tomorrow "and do that *Endgame* thing."

Eighteen years later, after writing a book on Beckett inspired by our prison tour (Homan 1984) and having sent a copy to John, a gift for this man who taught me about the relationship between actor and audience, I was thinking about him and that Cross City performance on the long drive back from a prison outside of Panama City. This had been my first such visit since the *Godot* tour, a request from a progressive warden to the Speaker's Bureau of the Florida Humanities Council for a "humanist," as we are called by that agency, to do a program for the inmates.

That visit had invariably stirred up all sorts of memories and feelings about theater in the prisons. I had had a productive two hours with the inmates: using them as volunteers, we had worked up a little production of Beckett's "dramaticule" *Come and Go* which then became a springboard for discussion. As the warden walked me to the gate, he thanked me for "coming all the way up here from that college town [Gainesville]." Outside of traveling evangelists I had been the first visitor to come to the prison in five years. "No one much gets out here, you know. We're really in the boonies. And, besides, there's been so many cuts in rehabilitation that we don't have money to bring in visitors like you." We laughed as we reminded each other that the Florida Humanities Council program was free of charge; all that the host had to provide was the space. Driving home, I thought of his comments and then of John.

A month later I applied to the FHC for a second grant. This time I proposed a one-week tour of the prisons with Strike Force, the improv troupe that I inherited when I took on a joint appointment in the University of Florida's Theater Department. Strike Force's charge was to raise important issues through theater. With a company of some sixty students, we did just that, through *Saturday Night Live*-style skits and improvisations, with a heavy emphasis on comedy and satire, though we were not above doing some very serious pieces. The company had several gifted young writers, and also developed material through our weekly workshops. Apolitical, seeing nothing as sacred, happily ranging from the socially provocative to the sexually gross, we had developed a rather popular "product," a stable of skits that could be tailored for the occasion. Over the years we had given full-length shows in theaters, a yearly production called *A Revue with a View for You*, benefits, performances in the university's residence halls and on the plaza in front of the library; we appeared at other colleges, before civic and social clubs, at university functions, in classes, in the public schools.

After several meetings with officials of the State Bureau of Prisons in Tallahassee it was decided that we should prepare skits based on issues of concern to both inmates and prison administrators, some two hours' worth so that we could then adjust the actual program for the individual facility. There were skits on safe sex, authority figures, divorce, being different, celebrating diversity, the physically challenged, love, friendship, skits on the minutiae of everyday life from being stuck on an elevator to embarrassment at a noisy relative, from an awkward man on his first date to surly waiters, ways not to approach an employer, little dramas arguing both sides of an issue, sketches on personality types, political figures, rock stars, caricatures of everything from greedy lawyers to overzealous cops, a monologue on rape. We had silly pieces, like one where a son has to tell his mother her feet are too big, and very serious pieces: four little scenes of domestic violence, escalating from a wife's accidentally spilling coffee on her husband to his stabbing her, all this accompanied by my singing that romantic song from *Casablanca*, "As Time Goes By." Minimum-security prisons with older populations would get a different program than a youth detention center; women inmates indicated special areas of concern; playing before an audience of lifers would demand a still different menu. We would visit some fifteen prisons all about the state, ranging from minimum- to maximum-security, giving twenty-two performances. At the larger prisons we would do two, sometimes three shows.

Strike Force was accompanied by an official from the bureau in Tallahassee, and he proved very helpful in dealing with reluctant wardens who, nevertheless, had been instructed to host the program. He was especially valuable in providing information about the personnel and character of individual prisons. Prisons can have very different atmospheres, often reflecting the personality of the warden, not to mention the nature of the crimes represented by the inmates. We were also accompanied by a reporter from Florida Public Radio, whose daily questions helped us with an ongoing assessment of our performances: what worked, what didn't; why we were successful here and less successful there.

Auditioning all sixty members of Strike Force, I chose four men and four women, trying to balance talent with maturity. From my experience with *Godot*, I knew that performing in prison can be frightening, that it is physically draining, that it takes a tough skin to withstand the insults, the taunts, the scare tactics that some inmates deliver whenever anyone, even with the best of intentions, invades what they see as their "home." Christopher Parsons, my Assistant Director, also came with us. We were a company of ten; I would be both the emcee for the programs and an actor in the skits.

Inmates can be an exhilarating audience. A population that has its own codes, its power hierarchies, its own demands that at once mirror yet sometimes reverse what would be the norm outside the walls, inmates make unique spectators. They focus on the actor with an intensity that in a regular theater perhaps only a handful of spectators can manage. A cynical friend attributes this to the fact that the inmates "have nothing else to do," that "the performance is a break in the routine." Having heard this judgment many times, I still don't think it even begins to approach the truth. Prisons are indeed given to routine and life is boring there, but my experience has been that, even in this environment where everything is decided for you, where you are powerless, where the "world" is purposely dull, inmates simply lower their threshold for details. They take in everything.

Our first stop was Florida State Prison in Starke, a maximum-security facility, home of the state's one electric chair, where almost twenty years ago the *Waiting for Godot* tour began. We were to perform on the basketball court, in the center of the main prison yard. There seemed to be a thousand inmates milling about; the guards made their way through men who suddenly became very quiet, then began muttering obscenities at us as we passed by. (One joke among the inmates is that prison regulations prohibit cursing.)

The routine turned out to be the same at all twenty-two performances. At first, only a handful of inmates would sit down or stand around the stage. The rest went about their business, talking in small groups, exercising, lifting weights, aimlessly wandering around the yard, all the while glancing over at the stage. Within about twenty minutes into the show, however, they would start to come over; soon we would be playing to a packed house, the guards silent observers on the periphery. Inmates are a noisy audience, but most of that noise is not disrespectful. As with our *Godot* audience, they were not passive receptors in the house but rather liked to comment out loud during the performance, thinking nothing of speaking to an actor onstage, making observations about the characters. Brecht would have loved this! Reality and illusion overlapped: one inmate, with guards following, even charged onto the stage to introduce himself; another, having heard I was from South Philadelphia, asked me, right in the midst of an introduction to a skit, if I knew so and so. Nothing escapes their attention, whether it be a frown from a nonspeaking character on the side of the stage or a dropped line.

By the end of the performance the audience, so aloof and surly at first, so distrustful, "wanted to be with us," as one of my actors would say. With the guards protesting, and then physically restraining them, the inmates would try to come on stage, to shake our hands, to ask about someone in the outside world, to make a further comment about a skit, exchange names. All the wardens agreed that this was a particularly dangerous time, and we were under few illusions about the inmates. Many try to con unsuspecting visitors; while glad that you came, others are not above getting your phone number for that day when they are released. An inmate applauding wildly one moment might just as easily slice you with a razor blade the next. Our roles were clearly defined during the performance; afterwards, this was not so. As a result, the moment we finished taking bows, and throwing "thank yous" to the audience, we would be surrounded by the guards and as a solid unit hustled toward the gates.

To the actor, we always wanted to stay longer, to do more skits. Prisons, though, are run on rigid schedules; the warden would always give me a clear signal when our time was up. Still, whatever their crimes, and Florida State housed many of the worst inmates in the system, we felt for this audience, *as an audience*: that is the operative phrase. Often, as we made our way to the van in the parking lot they would run along parallel to us on their side of the fence, calling out final farewells, asking that we remember their name, sticking fingers through the fence in the hope of some physical contact. We were always quiet on that drive to the next prison. I can think of no other word: there was a *sadness* present, tangible. It was always the same pattern: the initial fear entering the prison and making our way to wherever we were to perform (prison yard, chapel, cafeteria); the struggle to win over a reluctant, often resentful audience; then the thrill of forging a bond between actor and spectator; and that sadness.

There was also a clear gender difference among audiences. We played at two women's prisons in South Florida. Unlike the men who early in the performance would project an image of indifference or toughness before settling into the role of spectator, the women had no such need. They were receptive at the start, much quieter than the men during the performance, though no less involved with what was happening onstage.

With the best of intentions, one warden took us on a tour of the women's quarters before our show. We made our way among inmates as they lounged on their beds or dressed for the show. Later, during warm-ups before the audience entered, my actors told me that they felt ashamed at having intruded on the women; they were sure that we had offended them. Faced with actors who didn't want to take the stage, depending so much on our rapport with the house, I made a decision. Once the women were seated, I stood on floor level close to them and apologized for our barging into their living quarters. The leader of the inmates, a woman in her fifties with eyes fixed on me, came forward and, putting her arm around my shoulder, told me not to worry, that this "happens all the time," that she and her fellow inmates appreciated our concern. We then hugged, much to the consternation of the warden: along with the cursing regulation, inmates, for obvious reasons, are not to have any physical contact beyond a handshake with visitors.

The second day of the tour a major change occurred. That evening as I was about to introduce a skit at a prison in central Florida, an inmate got up and shouted out, "Do you do any improvs?" While we had done improvs in other venues, we had stuck to prepared material for the prison tour. The moment I said, "Yes," and before I could make any qualifications, another inmate called out, "Then do one of those improvs about Jody." Jody? The name was unfamiliar to me; I confessed so to the audience, who broke into laughter. An older inmate explained that "Jody" was prison slang for the guy who steals your girl while you are in prison, an obsession, as you might imagine, with inmates. I would learn later that the term "Jody" comes from World War II, Jody being the scoundrel who courts the wife of the soldier serving overseas.

I hastily picked three of my actors to play the inmate, his girlfriend, and the Jody character. Then I set the scene: the inmate, just released from prison, decides to pay a surprise visit on his girlfriend rather than calling her beforehand. Given the racial makeup of the prison, I purposely cast an African-American actor as the ex-prisoner. When he arrives, his girlfriend is making love to Jody. As he knocks on the door, she rushes out of the bedroom. Since the inmates had challenged us, I decided to challenge them. "Freeze!" I said to my actors, and they dutifully froze in position, the inmate having knocked on the door, the girlfriend waiting anxiously on the other side. I walked downstage to the audience. "Now, how do you want this skit to continue? Should she open the door? Or should she pretend no one's home? What do you think?" The audience promptly fell into a lively debate. We took a voice vote: the girlfriend should open the door. Hiding her nervousness, she threw her arms about the former boyfriend, glad to see him, surprised he didn't call, all the while casting nervous glances back to the bedroom where Jody stirred from bed, went to the door, listening, looking a bit scared. The audience howled with laughter, along with their usual spate of commentary from the philosophical to the obscene. The inmate character then noticed a sweater on the back of the chair, too small to be his. Another "Freeze" from me, and the obvious question to the audience. "It's Jody's sweater. Does she lie about it? Or tell him the truth?" An even more heated debate from the audience followed; the consensus was that she tell him she had bought it for a "friend." I called out "Unfreeze" and the actors resumed. Having decided to challenge the boyfriend, Jody came out of the bedroom. There came another "Freeze!" But this time it was an inmate who stopped the action. He had taken over my role! "Does she try to say the guy's her brother? Or does she tell the truth?" After a long debate, the truth won out.

The actors then played a very funny trio: each man protesting he loved her best, she flattered to have so much attention, the men then demanding that she chose between them, at length bonding in their shock that she could be such a two-timer. Another "Freeze" from a new audience emcee. I joined him in posing questions to the inmates. "How do you want this to end? Does she stick with her boyfriend? Or does she go with Jody?" Other alternatives were proposed, again ranging from the reasonable to the unmentionable. With an "Unfreeze" now coming on my cue from the entire audience, even from the guards who normally stood in silence at the back, the plot resolved according to the inmates' scenario: the men kicked the girl out of the apartment, had a few beers together, and became buddies, vowing to be careful of women in the future.

Now deluged with topics, we abandoned the prepared material, and did improvs for the rest of the show.

There exists an unofficial pipeline whereby inmates communicate with those at other institutions. The next morning when we took the stage in Orlando, an inmate at the start of the show told us that he had heard we did improvs the evening before and wanted us to do the same now. For the final eight days of the tour our show was drastically revised: half prepared skits, half improvs.

"Freeze" became the favorite part of the program. Even wardens joined in making requests. For the actors it was a tremendous experience because doing improv is a bit like riding a bucking bronco. You're fine for the first ten seconds, maybe a half-minute, but then, without a script, it gets progressively more difficult to stay on, to stay in character, to avoid frantic attempts at humor. All the time you are trying to keep the audience interested, trying to stay at the level of those easier opening moments. And in improv you are very dependent on fellow actors: monologues don't work, not to mention hogging the dialogue. You have to learn to set up your fellow actor, to appeal to his or her strengths. Now, if you do enough improvs, you tend to build up a "bank account" of lines and bits that work, that you can snip and paste into other skits. Still, coming up with jokes or good dialogue, especially for the more serious improvs, is a test. Unlike a play, an improv has no history with the audience, no gamut of audience reaction from past performances on which you can build. Further, on top of the pressures of creating dialogue, characters, and situations on the spot, the actor has to be doubly aware of what is happening in the house, along with being able to pass signals to fellow performers.

The first two nights of the tour, my actors after a long day would let their hair down and party. By the third night, though, we would sit up late assessing what we had done that day, practicing improvs from a list of potential topics, building up those bank accounts. Increasingly, even our conversations in the van traveling from prison to prison focused on performances, past and future. The variegated scenery of the state flew by, but we never saw the Gulf or Miami or Disney World or the hills of northern Florida. The tour itself took all of our attention; we had no aim in life other than to do an even better job at the next stop.

Learn we did. At our twenty-second and final performance an inmate told me that he liked "Freeze" because, "You know, it gives us a chance to be up there [onstage] with you, even though we aren't. To tell you the truth, I feel powerful being able to tell you actors what to do, where that story ought to go. Powerful. And I don't have too much of that nowadays. You know what I mean?" I knew what he meant. This different audience had taught us about the theater.

Eight days later, when we returned to campus, it took all of us a week to decompress. Our normal life of classes, even of playing before "straight" audiences again, itself seemed different, could no longer be the same.

"I Guess You're Wondering Why I Spoke?"

As an Artist-in-Residence for the Arts in Medicine Program of Shands Teaching Hospital at the University of Florida, I gave a two-hour acting workshop once a week for teenagers housed on the hospital's Psychiatric Unit. I worked in collaboration with Maggie Hannon, the recreational therapist, along with psychiatrists and physicians. Because their illnesses were so serious, these teenagers lived at the hospital, their stay ranging from a few days to months. There were schizophrenics, psychotics, young people suffering various forms of depression and anxiety, anorexics. There were manic-depressives. Some had been committed because of violence, or incest, or various other forms of abuse. More than one were the victims of self-mutilation. Removed from the mainstream of the hospital, the eighth floor on which the Psychiatric Unit is located is an isolated place, a world unto itself where visitors have to pass through numerous security checks. For the residents, trips to the outside are rare. Inside the Unit lives are regulated by a very strict schedule; for the teenagers, there is complex system of merits and demerits governing behavior. This system was even extended to my acting workshop. The more a teenager participated, the more points he or she received, points that could later be turned in for favors, from extra dessert to a trip to watch Strike Force perform.

On one occasion, in a private session with the therapist and one of the residents, I played a boy's father. The staff had finally consented to a visit between the son and his father, a man with a violent temper whose belittling and physical abuse had driven his son to three attempted suicides. Briefed on the father's history, I played him to help the son prepare for their meeting. It was a grueling experience. But such role-playing was the exception.

Instead, my acting workshops purposely did not try to make links between the theater and the real lives of the patients, nor did they directly use the theater as a "mirror" for the teenagers' problems, laudable as this function may be. Rather, I conducted the workshops as if the patients were theater students or actors I was loosening up for a rehearsal.

This conservative definition of theater, I discovered, proved useful to the teenagers. Whatever their illness or its severity, I noticed that the teenagers generally had lost confidence in their bodies and their voices. No longer taking pleasure in themselves, seeing themselves as "different" from normal kids, they moved and spoke tentatively. Fetal positions were common. Their voices sounded bland, purposely so, as if to commit themselves to any texture, any rhythm, to search for the right word, to convey any emotion through their expressions would somehow expose them to the very world, that "stare" of others they found so stressful. Whether on sedatives or not, they moved slowly, lethargically, as if putting a foot forward or raising a hand to gesture likewise put them at risk. I have had teenage children, know more than I want to about their style in speaking and moving, and also know how difficult a period these years can be. But these young people had no style. Unlike normal teenagers, they were not separating themselves from the adult world, defining themselves in opposition to embarrassing parents. Rather, they were afraid, and in that fear had withdrawn the body and voice, those extensions of the personality that first greet the world. A corollary was that they also withdrew from others, had lost even the most minimal of social skills. I learned from the therapists that there was almost no social interaction among the kids, except for angry outbursts when someone stole from or insulted a fellow patient. Many had been together for months on the Unit yet they barely knew each other. Each existed in a very private world, "a kind of Alaska," to invoke Pinter's apt title.

Nothing, then, could be more appropriate for such physical, vocal, and social withdrawal than the warm-ups, theater games, and exercises that constitute the acting workshop. For they are designed precisely to make one aware of the body, call attention to the voice, stretch the imagination, and develop an ensemble mood among the participants.

We always started with an exercise called "Names," where each person makes a gesture or some movement accompanying his or her name, something physical that "captures" the way one feels about one's name and hence oneself. Shouting out "Ted," a boy might spin around like a dancer; or "Cathy" could be signed with an outstretched fist. Once this is done, everyone else in the circle shouts out the name, along with its physical sign, three times. Afterwards, I would point to a particular person and have the rest of the group, on cue, make his or her sign. Thus, we would memorize everyone's name. With students or with actors meeting for the first rehearsal, given the reinforcement the sign provides to the memory, this is a good way to learn names. With these teenagers, saying each other's name, literally seeing how each felt about that name, was a small step in their thinking of something outside the self, responding to each other, developing that sense of "the company" actors cherish.

The first hour of the workshop would then be devoted to physical exercises: stretching various parts of the body; pitching an imaginary baseball while forcing an "ah" sound from the chest as the ball leaves the hand; swirling the tongue around the teeth and then the lips; tightening the body and then releasing sections one by one, starting with the upraised arms and ending with the toes; and so on. After that, we would do vocal exercises: jogging in place while making the consonant sounds to the rhythm, going up and down the vocal register, and, of course, all those tongue twisters and speed deliveries actors use to stretch the voice: the generic "Red leather, yellow leather" or my favorite, "The big black bug bit the big brown bear, and the big brown bear bled badly but he didn't bleed blue blood." By the time we finished there would be noticeable changes in most of the young people: bodies would relax, open up, voices would sound stronger, more committed.

Some physical and vocal exercises served as "transitions" to the second aim of moving outside one's self, developing a feeling for the ensemble. In "The Mirror," for instance, two actors face each other; "A" begins moving hands or legs, or the body, in some sort of graceful pattern, and "B" then imitates A. If A's palm draws near B's face, then B's palm does likewise with A's face; if B stretches the right leg, while slowly moving the left hand in a circle from the head to the hips, A mirrors the action. Now that they were working with each other, instead of individually, we could move to exercises like "The Balloon" where two groups face each other with twenty or so feet separating them. Each person in group A has a partner in group B. The As hold imaginary basketballs in their hands, showing the Bs, through mime, how big the ball is, how heavy, how it feels. On a signal, A throws the pretend basketball to B. The trick is for the B partners to catch the same ball as thrown to them. Then it is B's turn: the basketball becomes a balloon; then with A's turn, the balloon becoming a ping-pong ball, and so forth.

With the teenagers now more assertive physically and vocally, and learning to interact with others, we would move to actor's games that stress that dependence, that working in concert with others essential not only to actors but valuable to asocial, troubled young people. For example, in "Panel of Experts" five or six people stand in a row; the audience asks them a simple question: "What's the first thing you do when you get up in the morning?" or "What's the grossest thing you've ever seen?" Starting with the person on the left, the five participants answer that question in a coherent sentence, each person adding a word. Thus, if the sentence begins "The first thing I do in the morning is shake all the cobwebs out of . . . ," then the first person says "The," the second "first," the third "thing," and so on. The object here is to sound like a single person answering without gaps or fluctuations in rhythms, and with the common "voice" having a recognizable quality and texture. A variation on this is "Situation." Here the group supplies a person, a place, and an action: for example, an old man in the kitchen trying to slice a cucumber. The group then tells the story, each person, in order, supplying three or four sentences before passing the story on to the next person in the middle of the sentence. Again, if the group coheres, the story should make sense, follow logically, with the effect being that of a single person's providing the narration.

From here we progressed to actor's exercises that made even more demands. In "Translator" two people speak to each other in gibberish, with the person in the center supplying the translation: that is, the two speakers talk through the translator. In "Playing the Subtext" two actors are assigned six to eight innocuous lines of dialogue: "Hello"; "How are you?"; "Fine"; "And you?" They then develop a situation and a subtext. For example, the person (A) entering the room is three hours late for an important appointment, but B, who bends over backward in life not to judge others, tries to hide her anger; A, meanwhile, has purposely arrived late as a pathetic way of demonstrating his power over B who is everything in life A wishes he could be. Despite the banal dialogue, it is the group's job to guess the subtext, what is really happening between them.

The final exercise, "Freeze/Unfreeze," was the most difficult, and the one that the teenagers, once fully engaged with the world of play, enjoyed more than any other. It was a variation on the improv game we performed in the prisons. Two people get up and start an improvisation. At any moment, someone shouts, "Freeze," and while the actors do so by holding the exact physical position they were in when the call sounded, that person comes up and taps one of the actors on the shoulder. As that actor takes a seat, the new person assumes his or her physical position. When the audience shouts out "Unfreeze," the new actor begins an improvisation based on the present physical relation of the two actors, but on an entirely new topic. And so it goes, with participants shouting "Freeze" for a variety of reasons. Sometimes a particular physical picture will suggest an idea for an improv. At other times volunteers go up blindly, throwing themselves into the situation to see if they can come up with a new skit. Very often, the intruder would rescue a fellow actor struggling with the material, or having run dry of ideas. This last reason the psychiatrists found especially telling: the idea of throwing oneself into the fray to help another. The teenagers developed a good sense of timing, knowing when to let a skit run on, when to stop it, when to wait in the hope that those onstage would find their grove.

Improv, as I have argued before, is the hardest type of acting and makes actors very dependent on their partners. The best actors at improv develop a silent communication with their partner, know where the material is heading, steer each other away from dead ends, pick up on cues or suggestions dropped by the other. When it is most successful, improv sounds like a scripted play, and one that has been thoroughly rehearsed. When this happens, the audience's knowledge that the material is being created on the spot only enhances their pleasure in the playwright-like creativity of the actors onstage. By the end of the workshop most of the teenagers knew how to work together in this exalted fashion.

It was a teenage girl—I will call her Nancy—who showed me just how powerful and useful the theater could be. Nancy had been on the Unit six months and in all that time had never spoken a word. Severely depressed, having suffered unspeakable harm from her family, she had withdrawn deep into herself. She would always stand next to me during the workshop but never said a word. No one on the staff had ever heard her speak. She seemed beyond the reach of all. The other patients would taunt her unmercifully for her silence. Nancy was alert; that was certain: her eyes followed every word, every action of her fellow actors. Still, she never took part in the warm-up exercises, let alone volunteered as an actor in the games. It was an eerie situation: this beautiful, silent girl, there and not there.

Then, one day during an improv, she suddenly shouted out, "Freeze," her voice clear as a bell. Everything stopped. Therapists and staff silently formed a circle at the rear of the room; the other teenagers were stunned. The boy with whom I was working and I properly froze, as in a very controlled, decisive way Nancy rose, walked to the center of the stage, tapped my partner on the shoulder and took his place. We were so speechless the group forgot to give the cue to resume. I took up the slack: "Unfreeze!" As was the rule, Nancy began the new improv. Now, thanks to the prison tour, I had done a good deal of improvisation, yet am pleased to say that Nancy outplayed me. She was the perfect partner, setting me up, swapping cues, helping us both to fashion a funny skit. The group let us go on for five minutes or so, an inordinately long time to be onstage for improv. For the rest of the hour Nancy was up and down, shouting out "Freeze," gracing any partner lucky enough to be onstage with her. The other actors relieved her only with reluctance; she was that good!

The end of these Friday workshops was always a sad moment. The teenagers needed a father figure, and I, for better or worse, filled that bill. My actual leaving was an awkward affair. An attendant would stand in one corner of the room watching the teenagers, while another walked me to the door on the far side. There was, in effect, a no-man's land, a demilitarized zone reminding us all that they would stay on the Unit while I would go back to that real world outside the hospital. The kids would stand there forlorn, reminding me to "be back next week, OK?" One fellow even asked poignantly, "You won't forget us, will you—please?"

On this day, "the day Nancy blossomed," as a staff member described the occasion, I was halfway to the door when Nancy called out, "I suppose you're wondering, Sid, why I talked today. After six months. The first time since I've been here." I remember laughing silently to myself at her addressing me by the first name, for I was usually called "Mr. Homan" or even "Dr. Homan." I stopped in my tracks, turned around, and replied, "Sure, Nancy, I did wonder why." With her hands firmly on her hips, looking very much the confident young adult, she replied, "Well, you see, the reason is because this theater stuff doesn't frighten me . . . the way all the rest does. You know what I mean?" I told her I thought I did, but wasn't quite sure. She explained, "Well, you see the theater is real but not real. It's about halfway to life, just like me. So, it's real but it's not as scary as life. That's as far as I'm ready to go just now. That's why I spoke. Do you understand?"

I understood. Riding home I thought of my friend John who asked us to "do that *Endgame* thing tomorrow." Of the inmate who felt "powerful" when he took a hand in plotting our skit. And of Nancy, for whom the theater provided a stage on which she presently could meet life halfway. Different audiences. Precious audiences. Well worth an actor's time.

Notes

Chapter 1: The Playwright's Intentions

1. Tennessee Williams, *Tiger Tail*, staged at the Hippodrome State Theatre, November–December 1979.

2. A production of *2 Henry IV* at San Diego's Old Globe Theater (1963) opened with the final two scenes from *1 Henry IV*, while a 1983–84 production at the Indiana Repertory Theater (re-titled *Falstaff*) showed the events of the earlier play in silhouette by means of a dumb show behind a thin curtain. I saw this antebellum staging of *Much Ado about Nothing* at the Constans Theater, University of Florida, October 1993, complete with an African-American actor singing "Jimmy Crack Corn" for the merriment of the court.

3. Production of Pinter's *Old Times* (stage and television versions), directed by Sidney Homan, at the University of Florida, 1989. Cast: Stephanie Dugan (Kate), Sandra Langsner (Anna), Tom Pender (Deeley). Head of television studio, Don Loftus; Set Design, Sidney Homan; Lighting, Al Welhberg. I speak about this production at greater length in *Pinter's Odd Man Out: Staging and Filming "Old Times"* (Lewisburg, Pa.: Bucknell University Press, 1993).

4. Production of Eric Bogosian's *Talk Radio* at the Hippodrome State Theater, March–April 1988.

Chapter 2: Actors and Their Discoveries

1. *Uncommon Women and Others*. Produced at the Center for the Performing Arts, University of Florida, December 1992.

2. *Curse of the Starving Class*, staged at the Acrosstown Repertory Theater, March–April 2001. Directed by Sidney Homan. Cast: Pamela Greenberg (Emma); Ian Isom (Emerson); Nathan Kozyra (Slater); Bobby McAfee (Weston); Shamrock McShane (Ellis); Alex Scott (Wesley); Sharon Stevens (Malcolm); Kirt Taylor (Taylor). Crew: Stage Manager: Stephanie Chapman; Assistant Stage Manager: Georgia Adams; Costume Designer: Amanda Dinges; Set and Lighting Designer: Lowrie Helton; Assistant to the Director/Props: Christina Kinney; Dramaturg: Heather Staller; Make-Up Artist: Sharon Stevens; Assistant Set Designer: Christian St. John.

3. *Little Murders*, staged at the Acrosstown Repertory Theater, March–April 1999. Directed by Sidney Homan. Cast: Greg Hayes (Kenny); Lowrie Helton (Marjorie); Bobby McAfee (Carol); Scott Reed (Lieutenant Practice); Sheri Torres (Patsy); Andrew Toutain (The Judge); Desmon Walker (Dupas); Ed Zeltner (Alfred); Wedding

Guests (Suwanna Blakey, Heather Bruneau, Graham Cuthbert, David Johnson, Jake Seymour, Brittany Velasques). Crew: Assistant Director and Stage Manager: David Johnson; Set Designer: Ray Helton; Lighting Designer: Lowrie Helton; Props Manager: Suwanna Blakey; Fight Choreographer: Phil Yeager.

Chapter 3: Actors, the Set, and the Audience

1. *Galileo*, presented at the Acrosstown Repertory Theater, July 1988. Directed by Sidney Homan. Cast (Andrea Sarti) John Lennon; (Boy) Donovan Panone; (Cardinal Barberini [later Pope Urban VIII]) Kurt Orwick; (Cardinal Bellamin) Mathew Marko; (Cardinal Inquisitor) David Preuss; (Chaperon) Amanda Fry; (Children) Daniel Gordon, Daniel Homan, David Homan, Sky Muncaster, Tara Muncaster, Joshua Wood; (Christopher Clavius) John Lennon; (Customs Official) Kurt Orwick; (First Ballad Singer) Kurt Orwick; (First Senator) Mathew Marko; (Fulganzio) Mathew Marko; (Galileo Galilei) Andrew Gordon; (Lord Chamberlain) Kevin Main; (Loud Voice) Amanda Fry; (Ludovico Marsili) Kevin Main; (Mathematician) Mathew Marko; (Matti) Bob Freenman; (Messenger) Stuart Horowitz; (Mrs. Sarti) Marcia Brown; (Narrator) Marcia Brown; (Newsboy) David Preuss; (Old Cardinal) Kevin Main; (Philosopher) Kurt Orwick; (Prince Cosimo De'Medici) Donovan Panone; (Pruili) David Preuss; (Sargedo) Stuart Horowitz; (Second Ballad Singer) Mathew Marko; (Second Senator) Kurt Orwick. Crew: Assistant Director: Stuart Horowitz; Set Designer: Dan Hughes; Mural: Jim Evangelist; Lighting Designer: Douglas Hornbeck, Elayne Shields; Music: John Kitts; Costume Accessories: Michael Rogers.

2. Harold Pinter, *The Lover*, Constans Theater, University of Florida, September–October 1991: Director: Sidney Homan. Cast: Patrick Lennon (Richard); Abby Lindsay (Sarah); William Huseonica (Milkman). Crew: Set Designer: Dan Conway; Lighting Designer: John Wolf; Costume Designer, Connie Furr.

3. Production of Pinter's *Old Times* (stage and television versions), directed by Sidney Homan, at the University of Florida, 1989. Cast: Stephanie Dugan (Kate); Sandra Langsner (Anna); Tom Pender (Deeley). Crew: Head of television studio: Don Loftus; Set Design: Sidney Homan; Lighting: Al Welhberg. I speak about this production at greater length in *Pinter's Old Man Out: Staging and Filming "Old Times"* (Lewisburg, Pa.: Bucknell University Press, 1993).

4. *True West*, directed by Brian Rhinehart, Acrosstown Repertory Theater, February 1997.

5. *The Secret River*, directed by Sidney Homan, University of Florida, summer 1996.

Chapter 4: The Actor and the Prop

1. The tour of ten Florida State prisons was funded by the Florida Humanities Council for the fall and spring of 1973–74.

2. Production Note: Samuel Beckett, *Krapp's Last Tape*, Boston University, September 1971: Director: Linda Banks; Krapp: Sidney Homan. The Village and Santa Fe Community College, Gainesville, Florida, March 1990: Director: Sidney Homan; Krapp: Stephen Robetaille.

CHAPTER 5: BUILDING A CHARACTER'S HISTORY

1. Production Note: Sam Shepard, *True West*, Acrosstown Repertory Theater, March 1996. Director: Brian Rhinehart. Cast: (Austin) Tony Seales; (Lee) Paul Stancato; (Saul Kimmer) Sidney Homan; (Mother) Lara Krepps. Crew: Set Designer: Heather Seagal; Lighting Designer: Mary Apelski; Costume Designer: Susan Hewlett.

CHAPTER 6: PLAYING THE SUBTEXT

1. See Kathleen George, quoting Pinter from an interview in *The Sunday Times* (London) on 4 March 1962, in *Rhythm in Drama* (Pittsburgh: Pittsburgh University Press, 1980), 33. In staging these plays I found especially helpful: John Russell Brown, *Theatre Language: A Study of Arden, Osborne, Pinter, and Wesker* (New York: Taplinger Publishing Company, 1972); Elin Diamond, *Pinter's Comic Play* (Lewisburg, Pa.: Bucknell University Press, 1985); Martin Esslin, *Pinter the Playwright* (London: Methuen, 1984); Stephen Gale, *Butter's Going Up: A Critical Analysis of Harold Pinter's Work* (Durham, N.C.: Duke University Press, 1977); Lois G. Gordon, *Strategies to Uncover Nakedness: The Dramas of Harold Pinter*, Literary Frontiers Edition (Columbia: University of Missouri Press, 1970); Ronald Hayman, *Harold Pinter* (New York: Frederick Ungar Publishing Company, 1973); Richard Hornby, *Drama, Metadrama, and Perception* (Lewisburg, Pa.: Bucknell University Press, 1986); Andrew K. Kennedy, *Six Dramatists in Search of a Language* (Cambridge: Cambridge University Press, 1975); Austin E. Quigley, *The Pinter Problem* (Princeton, N.J.: Princeton University Press, 1975); Elizabeth Sakellandou, *Pinter's Female Portraits* (Totowa, N.J.: Barnes and Noble Books, 1988).

2. Production Notes: Harold Pinter, *The Lover*, Constans Theater, University of Florida, September–October 1991. Director: Sidney Homan. Cast: (Richard) Patrick Lennon; (Sarah) Abby Lindsay; (Milkman) William Huseonica. Crew: Set Designer: Dan Conway; Lighting Designer: John Wolf; Costume Designer, Connie Furr.

3. Harold Pinter, *A Kind of Alaska*, Harn Auditorium, University of Florida, November 1991; Director: Sidney Homan. Cast: (Deborah) Elizabeth Abbott; (Hornby) Patrick Lennon; (Pauline) Kristen Buescher. Crew: Set Design, Lighting, and Costumes: Sidney Homan. I talk about *A Kind of Alaska* from a different perspective with Elisabeth Homan in "'Dancing in Very Narrow Spaces': Pinter's *A Kind of Alaska*," in *Humanities and Medicine*, ed. Anne Hunsaker Hawkins (New York: MLA Publications, 1999), 289–95.

CHAPTER 7: THEATER FROM REALITY

1. Shamrock McShane, *Boston Baked Bean*, directed by Sidney Homan, various locations in Gainesville, Florida, summer 1994. Cast: (Track Coach) Greg Jones; (Football Coach) Paul Woodburn; (Athletic Director) Brian Rhinehart.

2. *Marjorie and Max*, directed by Mimi Carr, with Mimi Carr and Sidney Homan, Thomas Center, Gainesville, Florida, July, 2001.

3. Albert Gurney, *Love Letters*, directed by Beverly Thomas, with Beverly Thomas

and Sidney Homan, Acrosstown Repertory Theater, November 1992. Stage Manager and Set Design: Lowrie Helton.

4. I saw this production of *Six Characters in Search of an Author* at an off-off Broadway theater in New York, sometime between 1957–1959, but cannot remember the precise date, nor the theater.

5. William Eyerly and Sidney Homan, co-authors and co-directors, *More Letters to the Editor*, Acrosstown Repertory Theater, December 2000–January 2001. Cast: Ley Bragg, Lowrie Fawley-Helton, Michael Kelleher, Joshua Kim, Dave Morgan, Christian St. John, Terry Terpening, L'Tanya VanHamersveld, Robert Woods. Young Actors: Savannah Anderson, Julie Bonde Carolyn Booth, Mike Burt, Kay Costello, Dallin Edvalson, Ellen Frattino, Lain Healey, Amber Kerslake, Beth Ann Maslinoff, Megan McCann, Christian McCraney, Kenda McCraney, Clark Mitchell, Kit Niesen, Amy Roveli-Rix. Sheila Rowe. Accompanists: Emily Guey, Christine Shen. Crew: Stage Manager: Zack Holder; Set Designer: Ray Helton; Lighting Designer: Lowrie Fawley-Helton.

CHAPTER 8: PLAYING THE HOUSE

1. Wendy Wasserstein, *Uncommon Women and Others*. Directed by Sidney Homan, Center for the Performing Arts, University of Florida, December 1992.

2. *Boys in the Band*, directed by Lowrie Helton, Acrosstown Repertory Theater, August–September 2000.

3. I saw this performance in the summer of 1957, in Tulsa, Oklahoma, but—search as I might—I can find no records, not even a playbill from the production.

4. *Hamlet*, directed by Sidney Homan, Acrosstown Repertory Theater, March–April 2000.

5. Production of *Endgame*, directed by Louis Tyrell, Tampa, Florida, 1976.

6. Pinter, *The Lover*, directed by Sidney Homan, Constans Theater, University of Florida, October 1992.

7. *Zoo Story*, directed by Sidney Homan, Champaign, Illinois, summer 1967.

8. *Zoo Story*, directed by Sidney Homan, Boston University, April 1971.

9. *The Tempest*, Depot Theater, with James Hurt as Prospero, Champaign, Illinois, May 1967.

CHAPTER 9: DIFFERENT AUDIENCES

1. Production Note: The tour of the Florida Prisons took place in December 1992, under a grant from the Florida Humanities Council. Director: Sidney Homan; Assistant Director: Christopher Parsons. Cast: Christina Adams, Elizabeth Hermann, Mathew Herring, Mark Johnson, Lance Lucas, Rebecca Sorgen, John Green, Marlo Ward.

Pertinent Sources

Albee, Edward. 1974. *The Zoo Story* in *Two Plays by Edward Albee*. New York: New American Library.

Auberbach, Doris. 1988. "Who Was Icarus's Mother": The Powerless Mother Figure in the Plays of Sam Shepard," in *Sam Shepard: A Casebook*, ed. Kimball King. New York: Garland.

Barton, Ann. 1975. *Shakespeare and the Idea of the Play*. New York: Barnes and Noble.

Beckett, Samuel. 1957. *Murphy*. New York: Grove Press.

———. 1959. *"Krapp's Last Tape" and Other Dramatic Pieces*. New York: Grove Press.

———. 1965. "Three Dialogues with George Duthuit." In *Samuel Beckett: A Collection of Critical Essays*, edited by Martin Esslin. Englewood Cliffs, N.J.: Prentice Hall.

———. 1967. *Come and Go*. In *Cascando and Other Short Dramatic Pieces*. New York: Grove Press.

———. 1974. *Breath*. In *First Love and Other Stories*. New York: Grove Press.

Bogosian, Eric. 1988. *Talk Radio*. New York: Vintage Books.

Bottoms, Stephen J. 1998. *The Theatre of Sam Shepard*. Cambridge: Cambridge University Press.

Bradby, David. 2001. *Beckett: "Waiting for Godot."* Cambridge: Cambridge University Press.

Brecht, Bertolt. 1984. *Brecht on Theatre*. Edited by John Willett. New York: Hill and Wang.

———. 1985. *Galileo*. Translated by Charles Laughton. Edited by Eric Bentley. New York: Grove Press.

Brustein, Robert. 1992. "Waiting for Hamlet." *New Republic* 157: 25.

Churchill, Caryl. 1985. *Plays: One*. London: Methuen.

DeRose, David J. 1992. *Sam Shepard*. New York: Twayne Publishers.

Essif, Les. 2002. *Empty Figures on an Empty Stage: The Theatre of Samuel Beckett and His Generation*. Bloomington: Indiana University Press.

Feiffer, Jules. 2002. *Little Murders*. New York: Dramatists Play Service, Inc.

Genet, Jean. 1967. *Reflections on the Theatre, and Other Writings*. Translated by Richard Sever. London: Faber and Faber.

George, Kathleen. 1981. *Rhythm in Drama*. Pittsburgh: Pittsburgh University Press.

Goffman, Erving. 1957. *The Presentation of Self in Everyday Life*. Woodstock, N.Y.: Overlook Press.

Gray, Robert. 1978. *Brecht the Dramatist*. Cambridge: Cambridge University Press.

Greenblatt, Stephen. 1980. *Renaissance Self-Fashioning: From More to Shakespeare*. Berkeley: University of California Press.

Gussow, Mel. 1971a. "A Conversation (Pause) with Harold Pinter." *New York Times*, 5 December, sec. 2: 42–43.

———. 1971b. "*Old Times* Ushers in New Pinter Era." *New York Times Magazine* 18 November, 60.

Hall, Ann C. 1993. *"A Kind of Alaska": Women in the Plays of O'Neill, Pinter, and Shepard*. Carbondale: Southern Illinois University Press.

Hecht, Werner. 1960. "The Development of Brecht's Theory of Epic Theater: 1918–1933." *Tulane Drama Review* 6: 94–96.

Holland, Norman. 1989. *The Dynamics of Literary Response*. New York: Columbia University Press.

Homan, Sidney. 1984. *Beckett's Theatres: Interpretations for Performance*. Lewisburg, Pa.: Bucknell University Press.

———. 1989. "And Yet It Moves!" In *The Audience as Actor and Character: The Modern Theatre of Beckett, Brecht, Genet, Ionesco, Pinter, Stoppard, and Williams*. Lewisburg, Pa.: Bucknell University Press.

———. 1992. *Filming Beckett's Television Plays: A Director's Experience*. Lewisburg, Pa.: Bucknell University Press.

———. 1993. *Pinter's Odd Man Out: Staging and Filming "Old Times."* Lewisburg, Pa.: Bucknell University Press.

Ionesco, Eugene. 1989. *Rhinoceros*. Translated by Derek Prouse. New York: Grove Press.

Lane, John Francis. 1973. "No Sex Please, I'm English: John Francis Lane on the Pinter-Visconti Case." *Plays and Players* 20: 19–21.

Londre, Felicia Hardison. 1981. *Tom Stoppard*. New York: Frederick Ungar.

McDonough, Carla J. 1997. *Staging Masculinity: Male Identity in Contemporary American Drama*. Jefferson, N.C.: McFarland and Co.

McGuire, Philip C. 1985. *Speechless Dialect: Shakespeare's Open Silences*. Berkeley: University of California Press.

McLuhan, Marshall and Quentin Fiore. 1986. *The Medium Is the Message*. New York: Random House.

Marranca, Bonnie. 1981. *American Dreams: The Imagination of Sam Shepard*. New York: Performing Arts Journal Publications.

Mottram, Ron. 1997. *Inner Landscapes: The Theater of Sam Shepard*. Columbia: University of Missouri Press.

Needle, Jan, and Peter Thompson. 1980. *Brecht*. Chicago: University of Chicago Press.

Orbinson, Tucker. 1987. "Mythic Levels in Shepard's *True West*," in *Essays on Modern American Drama: Williams, Miller, Albee, and Shepard*, ed. Dorothy Parker. Toronto: University of Toronto Press.

Orr, John. 1991. *Tragicomedy and Contemporary Culture: Play and Performance from Beckett to Shepard*. Ann Arbor: University of Michigan Press.

Oumano, Ellen. 1986. *Sam Shepard: The Life and Work of an American Dreamer*. New York: St. Martin's Press.

Pinter, Harold. 1971. *Old Times*. New York: Grove Press.

———. 1981. *A Kind of Alaska*. In *Other Places*. New York: Grove Press.

———. 1987. *The Lover*. New York: Dramatists Play Service.

Rabillard, Sheila. 1993. "Shepard's Challenge to the Modernist Myths of Origin and Originality: *Angel City* and *True West*." In *Rereading Shepard: Contemporary Critical Essays on the Plays of Sam Shepard*. New York: St. Martin's Press.

Randall, Phyllis R. 1988. "Adapting to Reality: Language in Sam Shepard's *Curse of the Starving Class*." In *Sam Shepard: A Casebook*, edited by Kimball King. New York: Garland Publishing Co.

Reid, Alex. 1968. *All I Can Manage, More Than I Could: An Approach to the Plays of Samuel Beckett*. Chester Springs, Pa.: Dufour Editions.

Rosenberg, Marvin. 1997. *Adventures of a Shakespearean Scholar: To Discover Shakespeare's Art*. Newark: University of Delaware Press.

Sartre, Jean Paul. 1962. Preface to *The Maids and Deathwatch*, by Jean Genet, translated by Bernard Fechtman. New York: Grove Press.

Schneider, Alan. 1958. "Waiting for Beckett: A Personal Chronicle." *Chelsea Review*. 14, no. 2: 3–20.

Shaffer, Peter. 1988. *Black Comedy* in *"Black Comedy," including "White Lies."* New York: Stein and Day.

Shepard, Sam. 1981. *Seven Plays*. New York: Bantam Books.

Shewley, Doris. 1985. *Sam Shepard: The Life, The Loves, Behind the Legend of a True American Original*. New York: Dell.

Sokel, Walter H. 1989. "Brecht's Concept of Character." *Comparative Drama* 3: 177–92.

States, Bert O. 1982. *Great Reckonings in Little Rooms: On the Phenomenology of Theatre*. Berkeley: University of California Press.

Stoppard, Tom. 1980. *Rosencrantz and Guildenstern Are Dead*. New York: Grove Press.

Stropnicky, G. 1998. *Letters to the Editor*. New York: Simon and Schuster.

Tucker, Martin. 1992. *Sam Shepard*. New York: Frederick Ungar.

Wade, Leslie A. 1992. *Sam Shepard and the American Theatre*. Westport, Conn.: Praeger.

Wasserstein, Wendy. 1991. *"The Heidi Chronicles" and Other Plays*. New York: Vintage.

Zinman, Toby Silverman. 1991. "Teaching *Godot* through Set and Poster Design," in *Approaches to Teaching Beckett*, ed. June Schlueter and Enoch Brater. New York: Modern Language Association of America.

Index